Matthew White

The Affair at Islington

Matthew White

The Affair at Islington

ISBN/EAN: 9783744712118

Printed in Europe, USA, Canada, Australia, Japan

Cover: Foto ©ninafisch / pixelio.de

More available books at **www.hansebooks.com**

THE AFFAIR AT ISLINGTON

Fate hath no voice but the heart's impulse.
—SCHILLER.

BY

MATTHEW WHITE, JR.

NEW YORK
FRANK A. MUNSEY
—
1897

COPYRIGHT, 1897
BY
FRANK A. MUNSEY

THE AFFAIR AT ISLINGTON.

I.

IT was a rainy night, and the house was a poor one. But the members of the company extracted some little satisfaction from reminding one another that they had told manager Roberts how it would be, when he announced that Beverley would be taken in as a one night stand.

"I never saw a good show town yet," declared the first old gentleman, "that wasn't located on a navigable river."

He was talking with Marie Myrwin, the leading woman, just before the curtain went up on the second act. She scarcely heard him. She was feeling utterly miserable. The train had been late, and there was barely time for the company to swallow their dinners and get to the theater. As she did not appear in the first act, she had had it a little easier than the others; but then she had lost her trunk key, the dressing room was a vile place, and now, by the time she was ready to go on, she had a violent headache.

"I shall soon lose my good looks at this rate," she said to herself with a sigh, as, standing in front of the cracked mirror, she gave a final touch of the hare's foot to her make up. "Then half my capital will be gone."

But she had not lost them yet in any degree. Attired in the white evening dress of the ball room scene, the tiara of diamonds in her hair, she was a vision of loveliness as the curtain went up, revealing her to the few citizens of Beverley who had braved the storm to come out and see a play which—with another company—had made a record of a hundred nights in the metropolis.

At the first opportunity Marie swept her eyes disdainfully over the rows of empty seats. How humiliating it was! And what a disappointment the whole life had been to her!

It seemed as if she had never realized this

as she realized it tonight; and she had been in the profession for five years, ever since she was seventeen. The loneliness of it was its most oppressive feature. That excess of fraternal camaraderie, where everybody called everybody else by his or her first name, put out of the question, to her mind at least, any real sincerity of attachment.

She was thinking of this as she toyed with her fan and smiled during her by play with the first old gentleman, while the leading man and the soubrette were holding the center of the stage.

"Why didn't you brace up on a pony, Marie?" Harmon took the opportunity to whisper under cover of a laugh raised by Sophie Waters.

Marie gave a little shiver. Was it possible that she could allow herself to be spoken to in this way day after day and never resent it? But pshaw! How silly she was tonight. What could be the cause of it?

There was no time to speculate on this now, however. Her cue was coming in an instant.

She rose and walked toward the footlights, and for a second before she turned for her scene with Harry Vane, she scanned the first two rows of orchestra stalls, curious to see what sort of people this slow little town of Beverley turned out.

"Gilbert Dean!"

She did not even form the words with her lips, but the shock of the recognition was so great that it seemed to her as if she must have shouted the name. She recognized him instantly, in spite of the mustache he had grown since she last saw him, five years before. What a silly quarrel it was that parted them! How different her life might have been were it not for that! She had loved Gilbert Dean as she had never loved any one before or since, and now, as she saw him before her in the full glory of attained manhood, she realized that she loved him still.

"I must have felt his presence in the place," she said to herself, "even though I was not actually conscious of it. That is why the past has come up before me so forcibly tonight, why Harmon's coarse talk grated on me so. What a contrast between all those by whom I am surrounded now and *him!* It seems hard to believe I am the woman who developed out of the girl he once knew so well."

Had he recognized her? She could not tell. He had given no sign, and she dared not trust herself to look again. But even if he had known her, would he show it? It might be that he had not forgiven her, as she had forgiven him long, long ago. What could have brought him to this little Western town?

Her scene was over now, and she was back in the cramped little dressing room, where her costly robe looked sadly out of place with the rain discolored wall paper and the broken backed chairs. She sat down on one of these, and pressed her hand to her temples. How they throbbed, but it was not with the aching of her head now. Keen excitement, an infinite longing, possessed her. She must speak with him—must ask him to forget her pique on that night so long ago, must tell him how unsatisfying her present life was.

But how could she manage this? She might send the doorkeeper with a note around to one of the ushers, asking Dean if he could not come back and see her for a few moments during the next entr'acte. It would be perhaps a strange thing to do, and it might be that he would not come. Then she would feel more wretched than ever. On the whole, she decided that she would not try the experiment.

She tried to think of other things, and took up a novel she had brought to pass away the time while she was off. But she read the words without taking in their meaning.

"Of course he didn't recognize me," she was saying to herself. "I have grown older; my make up changes me, and then there is the other name on the bill."

She dropped the book in her lap, and sat staring out through the open door, at the chaotic confusion of disused scenery stored at the back of the stage. Just then the band struck up a waltz, one of the old favorites, to which she had danced many a time with Dean in bygone days. Every strain sent a fresh recollection pulsating through her brain.

"Oh, I must make at least an effort to see him," she cried under her breath; she thought how she would chide herself for missing this opportunity when it was past.

She hastily tore out a fly leaf of the paper covered book, and wrote with a pencil she borrowed from a stage hand as he went by:

DEAR GILBERT:

Do you recognize me in Marie Myrwin? I would like to see you again, in memory of the old days. Can you not come around to my dressing room at the end of this act? Yours,

ESTELLE.

Folding this into three cornered shape and pinning it together, she went out to the doorman and asked him if he would not send it to the gentleman in the aisle seat, center block, second row of orchestra stalls. Then she returned to her dressing room to wait, more nervous than before, for the answer.

But now her second call for the stage came,

and as she went on she saw the usher go down the aisle with her note. During her dialogue with Harmon she managed to watch Dean as he received it. She detected the start with which he turned as he felt the usher's hand on his shoulder, but then she was obliged to cross to a cabinet on the stage and stand with her back to the audience for an instant or two. When she turned around again, Dean was whispering to the lady beside him.

She was not a particularly pretty woman, Marie noticed with some satisfaction. She wondered a little why Dean had selected her as his companion at the play. The next instant she forgot everything else, and almost her lines, in seeing Dean rise and walk out of the theater.

She hardly knew how she got through the rest of the scene. She felt that he had come at once in response to her request, was even now waiting for her in the wings. How could she thank manager Roberts for playing this despised one night stand?

At last the curtain fell. Marie hurried off.

Yes, there by the door of her room stood Dean —tall, handsomer than ever.

"Gilbert!"

She just managed to breathe out the word, as she gave him her hand; then they were inside the room, his lips had touched hers, his arms were about her, and she was looking up into his face with all the restful confidence in his affection of the old, old days, that had seemed so far away an hour ago.

"Estelle," he said, holding her off an instant for admiring inspection, "how strange I did not know you till I read the note! I saw the resemblance, but never expected to find you in these surroundings. Ah, dear, how good it is to be with you again!"

"Then you are not sorry I was so bold as to send for you?" she asked, half timidly. "You —you have not forgotten how we parted?"

"That was when we were boy and girl, Estelle," he answered gravely. "It was a childish sensitiveness that separated us. But tell me about yourself. How did you come to go on the stage?"

"Papa lost his money after we went away from Lakefield. Then he died, and I must do something. I was reckless, having lost you, and craved excitement. One of my schoolmates had made a success in light comedy, so I went to a manager and asked him if he couldn't start me. And this is as far as I have got in the five years."

"Then you don't care for the life?" Dean said eagerly.

"Care for it? I hate it. You do not know, none can know but we who have lived it, the miserable substitute for satisfaction that is got out of our profession. To feel that I am the mere puppet to amuse others, that I must put my arms around the neck of men for whom I don't care a fig, must smile and jest when my heart is black with gloom; and beyond all to realize that the world, whether rightly or wrongly, holds me without the pale of respectable society, and gives me of its smiles only when the orchestra pit is between us—all this is too galling to be offset by the glitter and the glare that the audience sees.

But why am I wasting the precious minutes lamenting my lot? Tell me of yourself, Gilbert. How came you to be in Beverley?"

"Simply traveling, and stopped here over night to break the journey. How fortunate that I did, now that I have met you here! I never expected to see you again, Estelle."

"I never meant that you should, Gilbert. Our paths have trended too far apart. You should not be here now, perhaps, and yet when I saw your dear face, islanded like a welcoming oasis in that desert of strangers, I could not resist sending to see if you would come. This little talk will help me much in the days that lie before me."

"But I shall see you again, Estelle, surely—tomorrow. How long do you stay here?"

"We leave the first thing in the morning, so you see I must say good by now."

She tried to speak bravely, but though there was a smile on her lips there was almost despair in her eyes. She knew now that Gilbert Dean was not going to say, as she had hoped for a moment that he would: "Do not live this life another day. Throw up your engagement, and be that which you should have been years ago—my wife." What if he were already married? The thought now occurred to her for the first time. He had started to reply to the information she gave him, after a brief hesitation, when she exclaimed, "Gilbert, tell me something."

"Well?" he queried, smiling down at her, while she paused for an instant, gaining courage to go on. She was thinking of that plain woman who sat beside him.

At this moment there was a knock at the door.

"Miss Myrwin," called out the stage manager, "you must take your cue."

She flung herself on his breast. "Good by, Gilbert," she half sobbed; then she sped away into the wings.

II.

"YOU missed quite a good deal of the third act, Gilbert. What detained you so long?"

"Oh, an old acquaintance happened to spot me, and couldn't rest till he'd had me out for a chat. Funny I should run across him away out here, isn't it?"

Dean picked up the opera glasses from his wife's lap, and leveled them at Harry Vane, not because he cared particularly about seeing the leading juvenile at closer range, but because he felt a flush rising to his cheeks, and wished to conceal it in so far as might be possible. He was not accustomed to lying. His nerves still tingled from his interview with the woman he had thought dead in his affections long ago. He was dazed, feeling the ground of respectability slipping out from under his feet.

She was on the stage now, talking badinage with Vane, a vapid looking fellow with pale blue eyes and a weak voice. How beautiful she looked, and how unhappy she was! How unhappy Dean was himself! And yet, fifteen minutes before, he had been passively contented. Two years previous he had married a girl he did not love, to please his mother. He had thought it no particular wrong at the time. The girl was very fond of him; he loved no one else; it seemed to him that his capacity for loving had been taken away from him when Estelle Osgood went out of his life.

And yet he had not regarded this attachment as so very serious. He was only nineteen when they quarreled and parted. He simply realized that it seemed impossible for him, as a man, to care for other girls as the boy had cared for Estelle. So he had made two people very happy by proposing to Louise Dartmouth, who brought him a wealth of affection and an opening in her father's establishment at Islington that made him looked up to as one of the rich men of the town.

He had been—he was—greatly respected as well. It was the consciousness of this fact that caused his brain to seethe now as he recalled what he had done. And yet, as he watched Estelle Osgood move about the stage, listened to the enchanting tones of her voice, realized that he possessed the power to draw out its tenderest chords—he felt that were he once more permitted to decide, he must do just as he had done.

And yet all the while he recognized the hideous wrong of it. He even took a morbid satisfaction in viewing the affair on all its most abhorrent sides. This for a time; then he began to justify himself. Surely, he reasoned, a man had a right to go to see an old friend, to kiss her even. He was certain he knew of many respected husbands who kissed women who were neither their wives nor their sisters. How absurd in him to try to deceive Louise about it! Why had he not frankly shown her the note and told her that this might be his only opportunity to see a friend of his youth? She might even have gone back with him; she would have been interested in penetrating that usually forbidden region.

And at this point the other reaction set in. He knew that he would not have dared ask Louise to go with him; that he did not want her to see his meeting with Estelle, because, from the first instant that he realized she was before him on the stage, he was conscious that he loved her as he never had loved, never could love, his wife.

"Why don't you applaud, Gilbert? I can make no sort of noise with these gloves on. That little soubrette is very cute, isn't she?"

"Yes—oh, yes," he answered mechanically, and began to clap just as the others ceased.

He wondered why his wife did not see that he was terribly distraught. He was so unused to dissimulating. He recalled Sydney Rollins, his chum at college. What an adept he was in the art! "The Two Poles," he and Rollins had been called by their classmates, they were so opposed to each other in their tastes and habits. Dean had never been in a "scrape"; Rollins was scarcely ever out of one. What if Syd knew of this Estelle Osgood incident in Dean's life? Dean felt that he would almost be willing to tell him for the sake of hearing the ejaculation of amazement it would elicit. Rollins was a bachelor still.

"Too many loves for me ever to settle down with a wife," he would say recklessly, and yet Dean could not imagine him doing what he himself had just done; and with this thought he began to conceive a horror of himself, to liken himself to the sleek hypocrites in long coats and white ties who bring discredit upon the church whose banner they are supposed to uphold.

"Am I like these?" he almost cried out in utter loathing; and then the curtain fell on the third act, and his wife began to ask him how he enjoyed the play.

"How do you like Marie Myrwin?" she went on, luckily not waiting for him to express an opinion. "Rather stagy, don't you think?"

As the play drew toward its close, Dean caught himself wondering if the farewell glimpse of Estelle he had as the curtain fell, would be the last time he would ever see her. At this thought every fiber in his heart rebelled. He could almost feel the impress of her lips upon his own yet. To think that he would never again know the sweet sensation was maddening. He had made no appointment with her; had never even asked to what town she going next. His brain reeled. He was torn between the conflicting elements of love and self respect. And in the midst of the conflict the curtain fell, with her eyes fixed on his as she formed the central figure in the final tableau.

As Dean put away the opera glasses, and placed his wife's wrap about her shoulders, it seemed to him as if he were preparing to leave paradise.

"I've enjoyed it very much, Gilbert," said Louise, as they walked back to their hotel. "It was ever so good of you to bring me. I know you don't care much for this sort of thing."

Each word was a stab for Dean, and yet before he slept that night he was hoping desperately that the "Borrowed Plumes" company would embark the next morning for Kansas City, their own destination. In fact, when he came to think the matter over, he could not see very well how they could be going anywhere else. He remembered noticing the low comedian on their train the day before, so they were not bound westward.

"I shall see her again!"

These words repeated themselves over and over in Dean's mind. That he would be able to speak with her he had no hope. He was not sure that he wished to do so; he was not sure that he could live without doing so.

III.

THE Deans were late in reaching the station the next morning, and had barely time to step aboard the train before it started. Dean glanced hurriedly up and down the platform, but saw no sign of the players. Very likely Estelle was still in Beverley. They took chairs in the second parlor car, and Louise began to chat about some friends in Kansas City.

"Do you think we had better telegraph them we are coming," she said, "or just drop in and surprise them?"

"Oh—er—what is that, Louise?"

Dean was thinking that he was by no means certain that Estelle was not on this train. Nearly every one had been aboard by the time he reached the station. He was wondering what excuse he could make for walking through the cars.

Louise repeated her question, and still Dean was helpless. His mind was so filled with Estelle that it was impossible for him to admit any other topic at short notice.

"I don't know, my dear," he said at length. "I never was good at conundrums."

"Gilbert," exclaimed Louise, turning on him reproachfully, "what has come over you this morning?"

"Haskell, I guess," he replied, trying to laugh it off. "The fellow I was telling you of last night. I think I saw him get on one of the rear cars. I'd like him to know you. I'll go and hunt him up."

Dean was amazed at himself. How easily he talked of this subterfuge! He had not seen Haskell; the idea of using him as an excuse for making a tour of inspection occurred to him in a flash.

"You will be back directly, Gilbert?"

"Yes, dear," and he was gone. He seemed to be as helpless as a straw caught in the eddy of a stream that is sweeping it onward to the rapids.

"And that is where I am being swept," he muttered, as he passed through the vestibule into the car behind.

But he did not hesitate; swiftly he walked down the aisle of the common coach, eagerly scanning the faces on either side. He recognized several as belonging to the "Borrowed Plumes" company, but Estelle was not among them. Nor was she in any of the three rear cars.

"It can't be that she remained behind," he said to himself, as he went back to his own car. "It is very odd."

"Well, did you find Mr. Haskell?" asked Louise.

"No; I must have been mistaken."

He tried to think of something else to say, but the words which would come most readily to his tongue were, "What a hypocrite I am!" And yet, with the full realization of this fact, he could scarcely sit quiet, from the impatience that possessed him to ascertain if Estelle were anywhere else on the train.

He tried to think that this would satisfy him, that he could then return to his wife, and be at ease for the remainder of the journey. But he knew very well that it would not be so; knew that if he saw Estelle he could no more refrain from speaking to her than he could still the throbbing of his pulse.

For a while he tried to chat with Louise about her friends in Kansas City. He caught himself hoping that she would wish to stay there a while. The company would play in a city of that size for three nights at least.

Finally, he could control his impatience no longer.

"If you don't mind, my dear," he said, taking a cigar from his pocket, "I shall go forward and smoke for a few minutes. Amuse yourself with this," and he bought a book from the train boy, who had just made his appearance.

"Don't be long, Gilbert;" and as Dean noted the glance she sent after him, and realized that as yet it was all of affection and not of suspicion, he despised himself for his weakness. Nevertheless, he kept straight on past the smoking compartment and entered the coach ahead.

IV.

HE did not see Estelle at first, for the reason that she was so close to him, just at his right in the first chair from the sofa. He sat down on this, and bending slightly forward, said softly, "Estelle!"

She was too well trained an actress to appear startled. She turned around in her chair, and replied simply:

"Why, Gilbert, you here!"

But Dean could see in her eyes the great joy his coming gave her, and from that moment he knew that he would be reckless of consequences.

"I was afraid you were not on the train," he began. "I have been looking for you."

"How comes it you are here?" she rejoined.

"It is a happy coincidence. You see we are on our way home to——"

He stopped quickly, realizing from the look in her eyes that he had betrayed himself by that little pronoun " we."

" Then you are married," she said. " I wanted to ask you last night, but there was no time. You are very happy, I suppose."

What beautiful eyes she had! And she fixed them on him now with a wistful expression that went straight to his heart, and made him long to rise up just where he was, clasp her to him, and cry out to all the world: " This woman belongs to me by all the prior rights of love. Who says that we must keep apart?" For although her words were " You are very happy," he saw that she was thinking " How happy she must be," and the thought that Estelle was hungering for the devotion he had no right to give her well nigh drove him mad. By a powerful effort he controlled himself, and answered: " I am accounted a very fortunate man in Islington, where I live."

For an instant there was silence between them. Just then the train slowed up a little, and they had quite a distinct glimpse of a tiny cottage by the track. There was an arch of honeysuckle over the porch, and framed by it now stood a young girl. A sturdy fellow in overalls, and with a tin pail in his hand, stood on the steps beneath her, and an instant before the picture was blotted from the view of those two on the express the girl bent down and kissed him.

"Love in a cottage *is* sweet," Dean leaned forward to whisper. The whisper ended in a half sigh.

"My poor boy," said Estelle, "you are *not* happy."

"How can I be happy," he replied passionately, "when I have missed having you to make me so?"

"But, Gilbert, you have no right to say that to me."

"Yes, I have a right," he went on doggedly. "I want you to know, Estelle, that I did not marry for love, but to please my family, and —and because I thought I could never really care for any woman again after losing you."

"Please, Gilbert! Don't you see—don't you realize that you are making it very hard for both of us?"

"But it seems so unjust, so cruel," he went on blindly; "and if we can obtain some little satisfaction out of talking of what might have been, may we not allow ourselves that?"

"No, dear; because you risk too much. For me it does not matter so greatly; I am only an actress."

"For the love of heaven, Estelle," he pleaded, "don't speak of yourself in that strain. You will make me rail more fiercely at fate than ever, to think I am not permitted always to be with you, to protect you from the affronts to which you must be exposed. Tell me, when you play in the large cities, who goes with you from the theater to the hotel?"

"Oh, sometimes one of the company, sometimes another. It depends on what other engagements they have."

"And I suppose when they all happen to have these engagements you go alone?" Dean interjected, gnawing at the ends of his mustache.

"It has happened that way sometimes," Estelle admitted.

Dean ground his heel into the carpet.

"And must I feel that it will happen again," he muttered; "realize that, much as I care for you, I am powerless to give you the protection you need?"

Estelle looked into his eyes; there were tears in her own.

"I fear," she murmured, "that just now I stand more in need of protection from you than from any one else."

"What do you mean?" he asked quickly.

"If I had known you were married, Gilbert, I would not have sent for you last night. It was not right for you to come, to—to greet me as you did."

"Heaven help us, Estelle. I could not have done otherwise."

She raised her hand in protest.

"Do not make it harder for me than it is, Gilbert. Ever since I have found out that you were bound to another, oh, how earnestly I have wished I had not seen you again!"

He bent forward eagerly, and barely restrained himself from snatching her hand.

"Don't say that, dear," he murmured beseechingly. "Full of torture as our position is, I would not have missed knowing what I know now for life itself. Think, since I have come to man's estate, I have not realized what it is to love till last night. Is that not worth all the pain of loving?"

"But you are playing with fire. Every syllable spoken thus is an insult to your wife. There is only one thing for you and me to do; we must not see each other again."

"You condemn me to unhappiness, then—you, Estelle, who have it in your power to make my life one long Elysium!"

"That is not true, Gilbert; not now, at least. Your wife stands between us. There could be no real happiness for us, however reckless we might be. You will forget me again, as you have forgotten me once, and I—I will forget you."

There was a catch in her voice as she added this last. Dean's heart ached for her. He was about to speak, when she went on again quickly, as if fearing what he might say: "Your wife is with you on this train, then?"

"Yes," Dean said. "We merely stopped in Beverley over night. She dreads the sleeping cars."

"And does she know that you are talking with me?" Estelle went on.

Dean flushed slightly.

"No," he replied; "she imagines that I am in the smoking compartment."

"And you are deceiving her on my account. That is not like the Gilbert of the old days."

"I am not that Gilbert. He was a purposeless, thoughtless boy. I am a man, dominated by a passion whose seeds were sown in those halcyon days which we never half appreciated. Am I to sit down calmly to my humdrum existence, and deny my soul a moment's true happiness?"

"But you made this life your own, did you not?"

"Yes, but then I did not know that you were so dear to me. I thought that the regard

I had for you was a boyish whim, which absence had caused to wither and die. When I think——"

"No," she interposed. "You must not think on this theme. You must not be with me. It is time already that you left me and returned to your wife."

"Not yet," Dean pleaded. "I may never see you again."

"It is not 'may'; you *must* not see me again. Good by." She held out her hand, but he did not take it.

"Not now; just a little longer," he begged, adding, with a smile, "A cigar would not be half smoked yet."

The smile was not reflected in her face.

"That you resorted to such a subterfuge shows me how necessary it is that I should not allow you to see me at all. Did you tell your wife why you left her in the theater last night—that you came to pay me a visit?"

"No."

"It will be all the harder for you, then, when she learns the truth. If any harm arises from that call of yours on me, I shall never forgive myself."

A weary look came into her eyes. She rested her head against the back of her chair.

"I can't allow you to blame yourself in this way, Estelle," Dean said. "A thousand to one I should have recognized you before the play was over, and gone back to see you of my own accord. And now I want you to promise me something."

"Yes, Gilbert. What is it?"

She wondered if she could endure the ordeal much longer. Looking down the dreary vista of her life, she was appalled. The only way was not to think of it. But with this man beside her, his very presence reminding her of what might have been, what should have been, the desolation of that which was, which would continue to be, was forced inexorably upon her.

"Promise me this, Estelle," Dean went on, "that if you are ever in any trouble, if there is anything in the wide world I can do for you—promise me, dear, you will let me know.

Who has a better right to aid you than your oldest friend?"

"He would have the best right," she replied, "if—if he were not more than a friend."

"Never mind about that. Your promise!"

"Will you go, then?"

"Yes."

"Then here is my hand on it."

Dean rose. "God bless you, Estelle," he murmured under his breath; and "I promise. Good by, Gilbert," she said.

Then he hurriedly went out, and crossed back to his own car.

V.

SEATED in the smoking compartment, Dean tried to restore his nerves to their normal tension before going back to his wife. But it was a difficult task. His interview with Estelle had convinced him of the fact that she cared deeply for him, so that now to love was added compassion. Over and over in his mind he repeated her every word; every varying expression of her face was photographed there indelibly.

"How brave she is!" he told himself. "May I have the strength to be as heroic a man as she is a woman, and do that which will raise, not lower me in her eyes!"

Even while this resolve was forming, it was all Dean could do to remain where he was, when he realized that only a few steps would take him into the next car, were Estelle was sitting—alone. Only by reminding himself that he was doing her will was he enabled to stay and smoke his cigar out. Then, resisting an almost overpowering temptation again to enter the coach ahead, he returned to his wife.

She was eagerly awaiting him, anxious to talk over a situation in the novel he had bought for her, in which the interest centered on a *mariage de convenance.*

"It seems to me," she said, "that they should have separated as soon as they found that it was really misery for them to live together. Don't you think that would be better, Gilbert, than constant bickering?"

"But that would be hard for the one who loved," Dean rejoined, his thoughts on an instance that was not in a novel.

"It couldn't be," Louise went on, "for, don't you understand, neither loved the other. They went into the thing with their eyes open, and both soon awoke to the fact that they were equally miserable. And I dare say this fiction finds many a counterpart in fact. It has made me realize what a happy woman I am. Why, do you know, Gilbert, it has seemed to me as if our honeymoon had never waned?"

"That is what all true marriages should be, my dear," Dean replied: "a perpetual wedding journey."

He despised his own hypocrisy as he spoke the words, but there was now in his mind a grim determination to be a true husband to Louise, to accept his lot as Estelle would have him do.

"Sometimes it seems to me," Louise continued, "as if I had too much happiness, more than my share. You know there are so many marriages where love, like riches, takes wings after the first few months, and flies away."

What tortures Dean was suffering! Contempt for himself, pity for Louise, anxiety and fearful foreboding for Estelle—all these emotions were commingled in his heart. He could scarcely command his voice to make reply.

The day wore on. When the dining car was attached Dean hoped he might see Estelle, even if he were not permitted to speak to her; but she did not appear. When he went to smoke his after dinner cigar, it called for the mightest effort of his life to refrain from stepping into the forward coach to inquire how she was. She had grown very pale toward the end of their interview, he recalled. But no; he must not go.

He went back to his wife, and they chatted over plans for some alterations in their house, till dusk began to descend. Then a silence fell upon them, and each gazed out over the dreary landscape of flat plains, with only here and there a tree, and scarcely ever a house.

"As monotonous as my life will be," Dean muttered to himself.

Would he be able to endure it? How far could he trust himself? "Till death us do part." This phrase of the marriage service came to his mind. He must expect no happiness out of life, only a passive submission to the inevitable. "May it be short, then," was the half impious wish that formed itself in his breast.

The train had been running very swiftly; darkness had just closed in about it; the lamps were lighted, making the interior bright and cheerful. Louise put out her hand to draw the shade and shut out the lonesome prairie—a jar, a crash, and instantly they were hurled from their seats. Women shrieked, men were white with fear. A wild stampede was made for the doors.

Dean seized his wife in his arms, and a moment later they were out on the ground. Shrieks of agony filled the air; a car, shattered into almost a shapeless mass, lay before them where it had plunged from the rails. Flames had already started, and it seemed as if none within would escape. And it was the first Pullman coach, the one in which Estelle rode.

Dean felt as if he were going mad. Seizing an axe he remembered seeing in his own car, he dashed almost into the very midst of the flames. In a frenzy he worked to cut away the imprisoning timbers, for now he saw her, helpless, but mercifully unconscious, close to him, and yet apparently doomed. It was a race between himself and the conflagration.

The man won, by a hair's breadth, and with the only woman he had ever truly loved in his arms, he staggered out from under the breath of the flames that an instant later would have swept over them both.

His wife was watching for him, and she it was who knelt beside his unconscious burden when he had placed her on the grass.

"My brave boy," she exclaimed, "you have saved her life; but she must not stay here. Is there no place where she can be carried and made comfortable? Gilbert, look about and see if you cannot find a house."

And Dean went off, leaving those two together—his wife and the woman he loved. But he thought little of this now. His chief concern was for Estelle's safety, for till she was herself again, till she looked at him with eyes that recognized who was before them, he could not feel that his act of rescue was complete. He knew that behind him he left a tragedy, for he had seen more than one dead body carried out of that shattered car; but one life was all with which he was concerned, and he kept on until he found a farm house, whose inmates he startled by his announcement of the railroad accident.

Checking the torrent of questions that were showered upon him, he quickly arranged with the farmer to bring a wagon to the scene of the wreck. There was a physician among the passengers, whom Louise had found out and brought to the side of the woman she had watched over faithfully during her husband's absence.

" He says that she will be all right, but she needs care and attention, Gilbert," she told him now. " She seems to be all alone. We will go with her to the house, and see that she is made comfortable."

Dean could as yet scarcely realize that all their plans had been changed so suddenly, and by Estelle, of all people. The thought that he had been permitted to save her life thrilled him, and yet, at the same time, inspired an awful fear. He was sensible that having risked so much for her, she was now more than ever endeared to him. Fate seemed determined to throw them together, to test them to the uttermost. How should he be able to conceal his feelings from his wife?

And Estelle herself? What would she think, she who had counseled so insistently that they two must not see each other again? Precious as this opportunity of being with her, of being permitted to care for her, would be to him, it must needs be a pleasure much fraught with pain to them both.

Louise had not recognized in Estelle the actress she had seen the previous evening. She was indefatigable in her attentions, her quick woman's sympathy going out unrestrainedly to this sister who had escaped so narrowly from a horrible death, whom her own husband had saved.

Estelle was unconscious still. Louise held her head against her breast during the drive up to the house, now and then gently stroking the hair back from the temples. It seemed to Dean as if some awful catastrophe were impending. To have Estelle so close to him and in trouble, and not be able to take her in his arms and claim the right to protect her, would be torture enough; but to realize that his wife was filling these offices, all unsuspicious of the truth, sent a dagger thrust to his soul, and called out upon his brow the heavy drops of anguish.

What would Estelle say when consciousness returned? How could he steel himself to see and talk with her before Louise as he would to a perfect stranger, which his wife naturally thought her to be? The tragedy of death they had left behind them, he told himself, was as nothing to the tragedy of life which might lie before.

VI.

HALF an hour later Estelle opened her eyes and looked into the face of the woman who had been with Dean in the theater. She shivered and pressed her hand to her forehead.

"It is all right," said Louise soothingly. "You are quite safe now."

Still the look of horror did not fade; Louise even fancied that there was a shrinking from her touch. But she set this down to the shock of the terrible experience through which the other had passed.

"You are not in pain, are you?" she asked gently.

Still Estelle made no reply, but her glance went beyond Louise, and flashed from one side of the room to the other. Here was the wife; the husband could not be far away. Fate appeared determined to test them to the uttermost.

"What is this place? Why am I here? What has become of the rest of the company?"

As the last question was put, it came over Louise where she had seen the woman before. An actress! But Gilbert Dean's wife was broad minded. She took one of the white hands in hers as she replied in her soft toned voice, which was her chiefest charm, "There was an accident on the railroad. You were brought to a farm house near by. Now don't worry about anything. My husband will see that you are kept in communication with your friends. He has gone to talk with some of the railroad people now."

Although Estelle's eyes were fixed on the speaker, she scarcely heard a word, except "my husband." "An accident," she was thinking, and then the wish came that she had never survived it. She had a horror of suicide; it was so cowardly; but then to have been spared the pain of living without resorting to that; to have been eased of this burden of love that must be plucked out of the heart—and yet still carried as a dead weight, on the soul—it seemed cruel to have come so close to this deliverance only to miss it, and in its place awake to an ordeal more bitter than any she had yet undergone!

And this was Dean's wife bending over her! But she must not see Gilbert again. She was all unstrung. She could not answer for herself now.

"I must get away," she said, and with the words she fell back on the bed, conscious for the first time of a numbness of body that made her helpless.

"Oh, no, no!" Louise entreated. "You must not move. You had a very narrow escape. My husband drew you out of the very midst of the flames."

"*He* saved me!"

There was a sharp, strange ring of joy to the words. A look of almost radiant happiness flitted into the face of the actress, only to die quickly out, leaving in its place death-like gloom. Louise could not understand it at all. What did the woman mean by speaking, by acting in this way? But probably she was still under the influence of the stupor into which the accident had thrown her, and was not accountable for what she said.

At that instant Louise heard Gilbert's voice. He was talking with the farmer on the porch. She would go and consult him. Going softly out, she touched Dean on the arm and drew him into the hallway.

"It is Marie Myrwin, the actress," she said. "Did you recognize her? She has come to, but I think she is wandering in her mind. She acted so strangely when I told her you had taken her out of the burning car. Did you find out whether she had any friends on the train?"

"They have gone on. There will be a train that we can take at nine in the morning. What—what was it she did that you thought was strange?" Dean strove to keep the anxiety out of his voice, but his lips were dry.

"'Did *he* save me?' she exclaimed; just as though it made any difference whether it was you or some other stranger. But then I suppose the poor thing scarcely knows what she is saying. If you have seen her friends, you had better come in and tell her about them. She was asking for them."

Dean was grateful for the dimness of the lights in this prairie home. There was less chance of his wife noticing how tightly his hands were clenched, with the nails burying themselves in the palms. To listen to Louise talk of Estelle in this way, was torture, convincing him, as it did, of the actress' distracted state of mind. What if, when he entered the room, she should stretch out her arms to him and cry " Gilbert " ?

" Coward ! " he muttered, apostrophizing himself, and with his wife, went into the presence of the woman he loved.

She was looking toward the door as though watching for him, but she did not speak as he came up to the side of the couch and looked down into her face.

" This is my husband," Louise said. " He has seen some of your friends."

" Yes," Dean went on, his voice having a

parched sound, as though it came from a great distance; "they have gone around by Midbury Junction. You can go on with us in the morning and join them in Kansas City."

Estelle was looking steadily up into his face. Hers was pale as death, and yet she had never seemed more beautiful to him.

"You are very kind," she murmured faintly.

A tender light came into her eyes. Dean dared not trust himself within range of its magnetism. Muttering something about having to see the farmer in regard to accommodations for the night, he hurriedly left the room. Louise followed him presently, and found him smoking as he paced up and down the scraggly path to the gate. She thrust her arm through his, and after they had walked the length of the path together, she said musingly:

"I have found another thing to be grateful for, Gilbert: that I am not an actress. So much simulation of emotions that one does not feel, causes one to lose the capacity for thorough appreciation of anything that befalls one personally, whether it be joy or sorrow. That woman in yonder, for instance, seems like a stone, utterly indifferent; and yet for this very cause, I don't know when my sympathy has been so warmly excited."

Dean was already anticipating the morrow; that all day ride with Estelle, with his wife in the party. And yet beneath the dread, was a fierce undercurrent of joy over the fact that he was not yet to be separated from her, would still be permitted to look into those eyes in whose forbidden depths he saw the only happiness life held for him.

At this moment the farmer's wife came running out excitedly.

"Oh, ma'am," she exclaimed, "the lady's took with a bad turn."

"I should not have left her," said Louise contritely, and hastened into the house.

It was all Dean could do to restrain himself from following her. But he knew that if he should see Estelle suffering he would lose all sense of caution.

"For Louise's sake," he told himself, "I must be the hypocrite still."

And then a new fear beset him. What if Estelle should become delirious and say things that would reveal all? The mere mention of his name would be fatal. Why had he not told his wife that he had discovered they were old friends? It was too late now. The mask had been assumed, and it must be worn until destiny should snatch it away.

"Gilbert!"

Louise had come to the door, and was calling him softly. Dean's heart stood still. Her tone seemed to have that awe in it which we employ when speaking of the dead. He was instantly at his wife's side.

"What is it?" he asked in a voice so husky that it was scarcely audible.

"Stay here by the open door and watch," Louise said. "I must see the woman in the kitchen. The poor thing in there is quieter now considerably. If she calls out again let me know at once. You don't mind, dear, do you? Think how grateful you would be for friends to be raised up for me if I was placed as this poor woman is."

Each word was a fresh stab for Dean, who already despised himself utterly. But "Go on," he said. " I will watch."

The next instant he was alone with Estelle, only the width of the room between them. But he dared not speak to her. His wife might return any instant. Still he knew that Estelle was looking at him, was longing for him, and yet fearing that he would come. It seemed heartless for him to stand here and utter not one word of sympathy. He remained in the doorway, looking out over the dreary prairie, yet seeing nothing but that on which he dared not rest his eyes. He thought of the tortures of Tantalus, and then, with a mighty effort, he sought to force his mind entirely away from this incident of a pleasure trip and put it on business. This detention would make them a day late in reaching home. He ought to telegraph to the factory. He wished Louise would hurry back. What an anomalous position it was for him, one of the principal business men in Islington, to be playing attendant on an actress he was supposed never to have seen till the night before!

This was the line in which he compelled his thoughts to travel, but at this point they forsook his leadership and branched off in a direction that caused his breath to come in quicker gasps. Why must he stay here in the doorway? He had saved this woman's life, and strangers though they were supposed to be, it was not necessary that he should always keep the whole width of a room between them. Indeed, was he not giving rise to suspicion by this very excess of caution? Arguing thus, and with the wish mothering the act, it was not many seconds before Dean had left the doorway, and was moving softly across the floor toward the sofa.

He was within a foot of it, Estelle had just opened her eyes as though instinctively feeling his approach, when Louise's voice sounded in the hall.

"Gilbert, you haven't deserted your post, have you?"

Then, as she saw where he was, she hurried

forward with the cry, "Oh, has she fainted again?"

The flush of conscious guilt overspread Dean's face.

"No," he replied lamely. "I wanted to see if she was sleeping."

But Louise's mind was too much absorbed in her patient to have room for surmises on a matter that would seem so incomprehensible to her as the possibility of her husband's defection.

"Yes, and you probably waked her up with your efforts to tread cautiously," she returned, with a frown at him and a smile for Estelle. "These men are all alike. Now go out and smoke your cigar, dear."

This last was accompanied by a little push against his arm, which was in reality a caress. Dean felt it there long after he was out under the stars; the sensation seemed to linger with the persistency of some poisonous sting. He no longer had any confidence in himself. The only refuge for him was flight, and yet how could he flee when his own wife had taken possession of the woman who had come between them?

Suddenly the gate latch clicked and a man came up the path. He stopped Dean with the remark: "I beg your pardon, but is this the house where Miss Myrwin was taken?"

Dean stopped short in his walk, and a jealous frown wrinkled his brow.

"Yes," he said briefly.

"Is she seriously injured?" went on the other.

"No; not seriously, but——"

They had been walking toward the house, and just then Craddock, the farmer, who had heard a team drive up, opened the door, letting a flood of light out into the yard, and in that glare the two men walking up the path recognized each other. Dean knew his companion to be the leading juvenile of the "Borrowed Plumes" company, while the latter exclaimed: "By Jove, her gallant rescuer!" Then he added: "You are a hero, sir. Bravest thing I ever saw done. I was in a terrible funk myself. Never thought of lending a hand to a soul. I suppose I can see Marie!"

Dean felt like knocking the fellow down at hearing him speak of Estelle in this familiar strain.

"I don't know," he answered. "I will call my wife."

The other gave a low whistle, which escaped Dean's attention. A fierce, unreasoning jealousy was burning within him.

"Who shall I say it is?" he asked.

"Tell her Harry has come to inquire after her."

Dean hurried inside. He dared not trust himself long with this fellow.

"Louise," he called, at door of the "best room."

She came to him at once, and he announced his errand.

"Well," she exclaimed, "I'm glad some of them had the grace to think of her. Miss Myrwin," she added, turning toward the sofa, "some one from the company is here inquiring for you."

"Let him come in," said Estelle eagerly. "Tell him I will see him at once."

Louise accompanied her husband outside when he bore this message. The caller passed into the room they had left, carrying his cigarette with him. The windows were open, for the evening was warm, and it was impossible not to overhear his side of the conversation.

"Take you away?" were the first words that came to Dean's ears. "Cert. That's what Roberts wanted me to do, if you were able to go. But I understood you were all broken up. Steady, there. Guess you're not as strong as you thought you were, Marie."

"Gilbert," exclaimed Louise, "he is trying to get the poor girl away! She is not fit to be moved. Why, she can't hold her head up. Go in and tell him so."

Dean waited for no second suggestion. While he knew well enough why Estelle was so anxious to get away from the farmhouse, it maddened him to think of her going with a fellow like this actor. Besides, as Louise said, she really was not fit. But when he entered the room he saw immediately that his interference was not necessary. Estelle had sunk back on the sofa, inert and almost lifeless.

"Hard luck, isn't it?" said the actor, turning to Dean. "She hasn't the strength to move. Well, I'll go back and report to Roberts. I think she has fainted again. Perhaps your wife had better take a look at her. Awfully kind in you to take so much interest."

This was added as the fellow paused on the porch to light a fresh cigarette, after Louise had gone inside.

Dean made no reply.

"By the way," the other went on, stopping suddenly as he was about to start toward his buggy, "haven't I seen you somewhere before?"

Dean's thoughts at once leaped to the wings of that Beverley theater, and instinctively he turned his head to see if Louise were within hearing.

"My wife and I occupied front seats at the performance last night," he said. "Very possibly you saw me there from the stage. I remember you very well."

"No; it couldn't have been there, because it was something in your walk, as I came out behind you just now, that seemed familiar. Ah, I have it; you were behind last night. I saw you as I came off. You were just leaving Miss Myrwin's dressing room. Of course it is all plain now, and very natural that you should be so kind to her."

Dean gasped, as he stood there in the shadow, listening to words which were quite loud enough to penetrate to his wife's ear were she paying any attention to them. And yet he could not beg the other to speak lower, nor could he deny that he was the man. The perspiration broke out on his forehead. He fancied that there was an undercurrent of meaning to the player's last sentence. Dean resented this as an impertinence, and yet was not the imputation true? Had he not concealed from his wife the real reason of his leaving her at the theater? Was she not still in ignorance that he was an old friend of the woman for whom she was now so assiduously caring? Dean knew not what reply to make, so made none.

"Well, so long," added the actor. "I s'pose we'll see you before long." With which parting shot he climbed into his buggy, and vanished in the darkness.

VII.

LOUISE insisted on passing the night with Estelle.

"She is feverish, and horribly restless," she told Dean. "She seems to have something on her mind that is worrying her, entirely apart from the accident."

Dean himself slept little. Hour after hour he lay on the sofa where Estelle had been, thinking, planning, regretting, hoping. His brain a wild chaos of contradictory emotions, it was small wonder there was no opportunity for that calm to prevail which must precede repose. One instant he was abusing himself before his conscience as the master hypocrite, recalling his subterfuge for gaining that interview with Estelle on the train; at another his head swam with a delirium of joy as vivid memory summoned forth that moment in the theater dressing room when he held Estelle in his arms and kissed her. What conventionalities, what sacred ties even, would he not trample under foot to obtain such another moment of bliss?

Then the picture would change swiftly. He would see himself back in Islington, serving perhaps, as he often had, on a committee of citizens to preserve law and order in the town. Or, it might be, he was sitting at the head of their pew at St. Michael's; or passing the plate. "Hypocrite" was emblazoned on his forehead as he moved up and down the aisles, and women drew their skirts aside from possible contact with him.

But once again the memory of that interview in the dressing room would soothe away the conscience pangs, and at last he fell asleep, to dream of those old days in New England when Estelle was the queen of his boyish heart, and it was no stain on his honor to do her homage. All too brief, though, was this vision. It was succeeded by one in which unseen forces seemed to be dragging him to a doom whose nature he did not know, but whose full horror was so borne in upon him that he awoke in terror.

Dawn was straggling in at the window. He looked about him at the unaccustomed surroundings mystified. Then, as recollection asserted itself, and he realized that Estelle had spent the night in the same room with Louise, a deadly fear took possession of him.

"Why did I permit such a thing?" he asked himself. "Estelle is not herself. There is no knowing what she may have said in her delirium. And if Louise should discover!"

He recalled scenes on the stage where the wife had denounced her husband to his face. His fancy even went further, and conjured up an item in the newspaper, made timely by its connection with the railway disaster, in which Craddock, the farmer, should tell how all the parties in the scandal had sought refuge at his house. But Dean forcibly put these thoughts away from him.

"It is only my guilty conscience summons

such specters forth," he told himself. "Estelle will be in our company but a day longer. Then I may suffer, but Louise need never know."

"Gilbert!"

Dean started guiltily as his wife's voice fell on his ear. But there was a smile of morning greeting for him and a kiss as he went up to her. He was respited yet a while.

"How is the—how is Miss Myrwin?" he inquired.

"She is better, I am sure, and able to travel, but she acts so strangely. She is so quiet and sad, and lies there and looks at me in such an odd way. Really, Gilbert, it quite made me creep. At what time must we leave?"

"At eight Craddock is to have the wagon ready for us. Is not—Miss Myrwin coming out to breakfast?"

"Yes; presently."

When Estelle appeared at the table, what a farce it seemed—the formal "Good morning" which she and Dean exchanged. Then "I trust you are feeling fully recovered," he went on perfunctorily, and "Yes, thank you," she replied. . Only for the briefest intervals did their eyes meet, and most of the talking during the drive to the junction was done by Louise.

"Do you know," she said, "I never met an actress before. Have you been on the stage long, Miss Myrwin?"

"Just five years," Estelle replied, and Dean, on the front seat with Craddock, knew the ordeal she was undergoing.

"And were your people professionals, too?" continued Louise, not out of curiosity, but because she felt that the other might think she disapproved of her if she did not talk. And Gilbert remained so obstinately silent.

"Oh, no. How dreary it is out here, is it not?" At the risk of seeming rude, Estelle felt impelled to change the subject. She could not talk of herself to Gilbert's wife. At the best, each moment was torture to her. There, in front of her, sat the man she loved, who had risked his life only yesterday to save hers, and yet she dared not bestow one affectionate look on him.

There was but little else said during the remainder of the drive. And matters were not improved when they boarded the train, for all sitting in the one section, as was natural, Dean and Estelle were brought face to face. In proportion to the joy Gilbert would have experienced in studying every lineament of that dear countenance under other circumstances, so great was the pain to look thereon now, and yet repress every thrill of emotion the sight awakened. And yet, with the inconsistency of mortals, Dean begrudged every mile that was covered, bringing them nearer to the end of that journey which would mean that he would see Estelle no more. But he could not part from her thus, he told himself. There were a hundred things he must say to her, many facts to be explained. After they reached their present destination, he would surely be able to contrive some way of seeing her alone.

Buoyed up by this hope, he was more talkative during the dinner which they ate together in the dining car.

"How long do you remain in Kansas City, Miss Myrwin?" he asked.

"Three nights," she replied.

"And shall you play 'Borrowed Plumes' all that time?" interjected Louise. "I should like to see you in something else. We are going to stay over a day or two."

"We play the 'Plumes' all the time," answered Estelle, adding, with a faint smile, "That's what the people come to see, because stars made a hit in it last season. They don't care a fig for us."

After they returned to their car Louise fell asleep, with her head pillowed on Dean's shoulder. If the morning had been a time of trial, the afternoon had been turned into a regular court of inquisition. One instant Dean felt himself to be a monster, realizing how fully his love was trusted by the woman at his side. The next he was glancing at the opposite seat, wishing Estelle would look up from her book that they might exchange one glance of mutual comprehension. But she would not do this, and at last he ventured to speak.

"That must be a very interesting story?" he said.

"Not particularly," Estelle replied, still keeping her eyes on the page.

"The other passengers will think we have quarreled," Dean went on, "if we remain so studiously indifferent to each other."

Estelle shrugged her shoulders.

"What they think is nothing to me," she answered. "Besides, our talking may disturb your wife."

"You are cruel, Es——"

He checked himself as she flashed at him a warning glance that thrilled him through and through. After an instant of silence he began again.

"Who was that fellow, calling himself 'Harry,' who came to the farmhouse last night? He seemed to know you very well. Have you been playing together long?"

"Only this season. He is really a very convenient boy to have at hand." Estelle closed her book, and began looking out of the window.

"Ah," said Dean. "I suppose he accompanies you home from the theater more often than the others?"

Estelle gave a little laugh, which Dean knew at once was a forced one, such as she would use on the stage.

"As often as his wife will let him," she answered. "She is half a dozen years older than he, and plays the first old lady."

Dean divined at once that Estelle was trying to disgust him with her by assuming the tone of a certain class of her profession from whom she was by nature removed an infinite distance. The effort it cost her to do this was apparent in the tone of the voice, in the sudden dropping of the eyes—in her whole attitude. A fairly good actress on the stage, she was a poor one when it came to deceiving the man she loved. So Dean smiled and shook his head, and said "Poorly played, mademoiselle," with as near an approach to lightness of heart as he had experienced for the past forty eight hours.

The halting of the train woke Louise, and for the rest of the journey the conversation was general, pertaining mostly to the country through which they were passing. It was dark when they arrived at Kansas City, and Estelle said she would be obliged to go at once to the theater, when Dean asked her at what hotel she wished to be set down. Louise had insisted that she take a seat in the carriage from the station.

The driver knew where the theater was located, and when he drew up at the stage door Estelle held out her hand to Louise.

"You have been very kind indeed to me," she said. "I cannot thank you; can only try to do so, but believe me, I am grateful."

Dean was already on the sidewalk.

"I am coming for you after the performance tonight," he whispered, as he walked the few paces between the curb and the doorway with her.

"You must not," she told him, giving him her hand. "Good by."

"I must see you alone once more," he persisted, "so it is *au revoir.*"

And he was gone before she could again forbid him.

VIII.

Half past ten that same night. The Deans' friends had made them royally welcome, but Louise pleaded fatigue as an excuse for retiring early. "Come, Gilbert," she said; "you must be worn out, too. You could have had no adequate rest on that sofa last night."

"I am not tired, dear," replied Dean, already perplexed as to the manner in which he could keep his appointment with Estelle. There was no parleying with conscience now; for the nonce that appendage of his moral nature appeared to have retired from the field. The only thing that worried him was the difficulty in the way of leaving the Fords' and getting back again. It would look odd to ask for a latchkey. Yet he had determined on taking Estelle to supper, and it would be too late to ring the bell when he returned.

He went with his wife to their room, feeling that it would be a simpler matter to get away from her than to give reasons to Ford and *his* wife in addition. He seated himself in a chair by the window, and looked down into the street.

"I believe I will go out and take a walk," he said suddenly, pausing in the act of winding his watch.

"Why, Gilbert!" exclaimed Louise. "How absurd, at this hour?"

"It is not late," he responded. "Only half past ten. I haven't had any sort of exercise today. I am certain I could not sleep without it."

Louise came over and put her arms about his neck.

"My poor boy," she said, "you have not been quite yourself since you went into that burning car. You know better than I what is best for you. Go and take your walk, but wait—let me go to Jessie and get a latchkey, that you need not ring when you come back."

Dean's conscience did stir uneasily when Louise sped away on this errand, but he stifled it by assuring himself that it was the last time; tomorrow they would start for Islington, and it was not likely he should ever see Estelle again. But he must bid her good by; have a few parting words which only they two should hear.

Louise came back with a relieved look.

"Tom says he will go with you," she announced. "He has been troubled some with insomnia, and thinks, with you, that a little stroll may help him. Now be sure you two men don't get into any mischief, and be back soon."

She helped him on with his coat, gave him a kiss, and then held him close for an instant. And he—he was scarcely conscious of any of those things. His mind was all astir planning means of getting rid of Tom Ford. Why had he allowed Louise to ask for that key? But he determined not to be balked of his design. He would find some way of giving Tom the slip. The latter was waiting for him in the lower hall.

"Glad you thought of this scheme, Dean?" he said. "We'll take a brisk turn of twenty minutes, then perhaps I can sleep. Let me see, which way shall we go?"

"Down town," replied Dean promptly. "I'd like to see a little of your city's night life at the heart of it. And come to think," he added, "I want to stop in at one of your prominent hotels and look over the register. There may be a man I know stopping there."

They started off. Ford talked volubly of the growth of his city, and pointed out various structures of interest as they passed them. But Dean paid little heed. He took note only of the fleeting minutes, realizing that if he reached the theater after Estelle had left it he would not know where to find her, as she was ignorant at which hotel the company would stay. He was remorseless in his intention to get rid of Ford; he cared not by what means he accomplished his end. In contrasting his present frame of mind with his normal one, he recalled Stevenson's story of *Jekyl* and *Hyde*. It seemed odd, he reflected, that love, supposed to be the noblest sentiment in the world, should be capable of so transforming character.

It was ten minutes to eleven when they entered the corridor of a large hotel. "'Borrowed Plumes' is not a long play," Dean was reminding himself nervously. "I think it was over the other night soon after half past ten. I haven't an instant to lose."

He was bending over the register, not seeing one of the names on the page down which his finger was traveling. He raised his eyes and glanced toward the door, with Ford still looking over his shoulder.

"By Jove," he exclaimed, in well simulated surprise, "there he goes. Excuse me a minute, Tom," and off he darted.

Once on the sidewalk, Dean strode rapidly off in the direction of the theater. Even while his cheeks flushed with shame at the ruse he had played on his friend, his heart was pounding away mightily at the thought of soon being with Estelle again. Although it was barely three hours since he had seen her, it seemed an age to Dean. He was panting when he arrived at the stage door. Already some of the members of the cast were leaving it. Dean recalled the fact that Harry Vane might see him, but he did not care. *He* would see Estelle—if she had not gone.

"Has Miss Myrwin passed out yet?" he inquired eagerly of the doorkeeper.

"Don't know her," was the short answer. "First night the company's here."

Dean had his hand in his pocket, to fee the man to let him step inside and look around, when Estelle herself appeared. Vane was with her. She frowned when she saw Dean, but having thrust aside so many obstacles in his path up to this point, he was not to be checked now.

"I have come to keep my appointment," he said quietly, offering his arm.

Vane dropped back, with a courteous "Good evening, Mr. Dean." Estelle took the arm and said nothing until they reached the sidewalk. Then—

"Why did you come?" she began. "Have I not already been tortured sufficiently?"

"And I?" he returned. "Do you think I have not suffered with you? And could you imagine that I could bear to part thus?"

"But think of the risk, Gilbert? Does your wife know you have come to see me? Does——"

"Let us not talk of others, Estelle, in the brief time we have together. I want you to go to supper with me, to hear you say——"

"No, no, Gilbert, I cannot. It is not right to try me so. It is hard enough as it is for me."

They were walking slowly along the quiet street which ran in the rear of the one on which the theater fronted. Lifting her face towards Dean's in the glare of an arc lamp, Estelle continued rapidly:

"Gilbert, what if right here I should throw my arms about your neck, should declare I loved you passionately, and beg you to abandon wife, home, friends, career, respectability—everything that has lifted you to the plane you now occupy—and come with me? If I should do this and you should consent, think you, Gilbert, that you would be happy, or I? Would not the specter of the past be ever at our side? Heaven knows, I am weak enough. When I recall what you were to me once, what you did for me only yesterday, what I know you feel for me every minute of the day, my heart rebels, but there is no appeal from the fate that has separated us. I am right, Gilbert. You must admit that I am."

"Even if you are, dear," Dean replied, "all the more reason that you should give me the opportunity to talk with you tonight. The present is ours. Let us make the most of it. You will go to supper with me now, will you not?"

"Yes, if you will promise that you will never try to meet me again, nor write to me even."

"You may trust me, Estelle, but in turn you must not forget the promise you made me yesterday— to send to me whenever you were in trouble of any kind, or needed a friend. You know where I can be found."

They had turned into the more brilliantly lighted thoroughfare, and as they strolled along till they should come to a restaurant, Dean was suddenly conscious that Tom Ford had just passed them. Had he seen him? There was no means of knowing. There would be time enough to think of that after he had left Estelle. He would not borrow worry from the future.

It was after one o'clock when they rose from that supper. Forcibly banishing all cares from his mind, Dean had enjoyed every minute of it. Estelle, too, threw off the restraint she had lately imposed on herself, and was the fascinating creature, tenfold intensified, she had been as his boyish ideal.

"And now it is, it must be good by, not *au revoir*, Gilbert," she said, when he had walked to the hotel with her.

"Unless you send for me," he answered. "Then I will come, no matter what there is to hinder. Good by."

A long pressure of the hand, a looking into each other's eyes in the starlight, and then

Estelle passed swiftly into the hotel, leaving Dean to walk rapidly away, his footfalls echoing distinctly in the silent street. But his swift pace soon changed to a slow one. He must take time to look his position in the face. In getting rid of Tom Ford, he had deprived himself of the means of reëntering the house without arousing the family. Then how should he explain to Ford the reason of his failure to return to the hotel? Most serious of all, what should he say if Ford had seen him with Estelle?

"I am not a clever scoundrel," Dean told himself with a bitter smile. "I think I am smarter in channels where brilliancy of ideas is put to more legitimate use. I ought to be a worse man or a better one to get any measure of content out of life. Perhaps if——"

But he still recoiled in horror from exposure. He had been about to tell himself that it would be perhaps the best thing that could happen if it turned out that Tom Ford *had* seen him with Estelle. There would be a scene with Louise, a quarrel, all barriers of self respect would be broken down, and he left free to be with Estelle as much as he pleased.

Walking slowly, he had by this time arrived in front of the Fords' house. He was on the opposite side of the street, and glancing up instinctively at the window of the room to which he and Louise had been assigned, he saw her there. The figure disappeared instantly, and a moment later the front door was opened. It was Louise. She had been watching for him, and had come down to let him in.

"I was so anxious about you, Gilbert," she murmured. "Tom came home hours ago, and said he had missed you in some way. Where have you been?"

If she only knew! For one instant Dean was tempted to tell her; to roll off the burden of deceit that was weighing him down. But why do this now, he asked himself? He was not to see Estelle again; the knowledge of the truth would only needlessly embitter Louise's life. No, it was better to let her ignorance remain bliss.

"Why, did not Tom tell you, little girl?" he said. "I caught a glimpse of the man I went into the hotel to look for, and he insisted on taking me out to supper. I told him about Tom being with me, and we went back to get him, too, but he had gone."

How glibly the falsehoods slid from his tongue now! The utterance of them appeared to give him no concern except that which was occasioned by the possibility that they were not clever enough. If Tom *had* seen him with Estelle? But the morrow's invention could look after that. Meantime, the sooner he got away from Kansas City the better.

"Louise," he said, "would you mind starting for home tomorrow? You know we have lost a day by the accident, and I feel that I ought to get back."

"I am eager for that myself, dear," she replied.

And so it was settled that they leave on an afternoon train. Dean dared not allow himself to think of Estelle. He knew that she was right, and that in flight lay his only safety. He expected to be unhappy away from her, but Louise, at least, would be left in the joyous contentment that had been her portion since the day he had asked her to be his wife.

Dean chafed a little under Tom Ford's eye at breakfast.

"A pretty trick you served me last night, Gilbert," he said rallyingly, after his morning's greeting. But there was a penetrating element in the gaze he bent on his guest.

"I beg your pardon, old man," Dean replied. "It was a shabby fashion in which to treat one's host, but then when I caught that glimpse of Holden just vanishing through the door I knew I should have to make a bolt for it, or lose him altogether. We came back afterwards to look you up, but you had gone."

"Oh, did you?" rejoined Ford dryly. "Very good of you. But I'll let you off this time, only it's too bad I missed that supper."

And so the subject was dismissed from everybody's mind with a laugh—from everybody's but Dean's own, and possibly Tom's. Did the latter know more than he thought it for his guest's best interest to admit? This was the problem that kept Dean in unrest all the forenoon. On thinking it over, he did not comprehend how Tom could well have escaped seeing him with Estelle.

He breathed a deep sigh of relief when he and Louise boarded the train for the East that afternoon. Although he had caught Tom looking at him in a peculiar way once or twice, nothing more was said about the night before. He and Jessie both came to the station to see them off. Louise and Jessie had said and kissed their adieux; Dean had gone to the back platform to give a final hand clasp as the train moved off. Jessie ran forward to the window in response to a sudden call from Louise. This left Tom and Gilbert alone. The cars began to move.

"Good by, old fellow," said Ford. "Next time don't call the friends you stop in at hotels to see by two names."

There was no chance for Dean to reply,

Jessie had run back to join her husband; both were waving their hands to him now. Dean tried to smile as he took off his hat in acknowledgment, but his heart failed him for fear.

He remembered now that while they had been looking over that hotel register together, Tom had asked his friend's name, and he had answered "Green." Then the next morning he had called him Holden! How stupid of him, and how he must be despised, Dean thought! He knew what would be his opinion of Ford had he caught him in a deception of the sort. He felt he was not worthy to even sit beside his wife when he went back to her. How long would she permit him to do this? How long would it be—or how short a time perhaps—before she would turn from him in horror as though there were contamination in his touch? And yet he had committed no great crime, he told himself. Surely he exaggerated the importance of his acts. Partially justifying himself to himself in this manner, Dean was enabled to carry his head erect and to deport himself in the dignified manner, that befitted his standing when they arrived again at Islington. It seemed good to him to get back. Here were the props to respectability that would uphold him in his determination to crush down the desire to see Estelle again.

IX.

IT was November. Dean and his wife had been back in Islington several weeks. Contrary to his promise to Estelle to forget her, he had thought of her more and more from day to day, and many of these thoughts were transmitted to her through the mails. Letters such as these she could not do otherwise than answer. Her resolution that day on the train was easily spoken; it was not so easily kept. Had he not saved her life?

As for Dean, he was looking forward with eager longing to seeing her when the company came East. "When shall you play in Albany?" he wrote her. "Wire me exact date."

He thought of little else than Estelle now. According to her last letter she would be in Albany some time in the following week. "This is Saturday," he mused. "A telegram should reach me by Monday noon."

Dean went to church with his wife on Sunday, but the words of the preacher did not penetrate his ears. In his Sunday paper he had seen that the "Borrowed Plumes" company would play in Albany on Tuesday night.

All day Monday he waited anxiously for a telegram from Estelle. None came. He was nervous, distraught, irritable. Could it be that she did not wish to see him? And after the letters she had written him!

"She *must* see me," he resolved. "I will go to Albany, any way." He went home to his wife with deception on his lips. His kiss was not the less sweet to her.

"Dear," he began, putting his arm around her as he walked with her towards the window, "I must go over to Albany tomorrow."

"Oh, Gilbert!"

"I'm sorry," he went on quickly, looking intently across the street. "I'm sorry, but I have just learned that Illford is to be there. He has a bill before the Legislature, and wants my influence. I cannot deny him the favor."

All Tuesday forenoon he still looked for a

telegram, but in vain. At times he was indignant, and wavered in his determination, but each flash of indignation was succeeded by a longing to see Estelle which there was no denying, and at one o'clock he was off. Louise's eyes followed him wistfully as he walked down the street. "I wish I had gone to Albany with him," she said to herself. "I wonder why I didn't think of it in time. I wonder why Gilbert didn't suggest it."

Towards night Louise was at the window again, and in her reverie she could see Gilbert as distinctly as she had seen him a few hours before on his way to the station. "There is not another man in Islington," she reflected, "with such a figure, and he is handsome— handsomer than any other man in town. I remember the day I saw him first. And it was all so unexpected. Suppose I had never met him!" and she sighed deeply.

As she stood there, thinking in this wise, a cab drove up to the Uptons', across the way. She watched as the coachman got down from his box and helped the occupant into the house. John Upton's failing was known pretty generally in Islington by this time.

"Poor Mary," murmured Louise, as she drew the blind, and turned on the electric light. "What if I had a burden like hers to carry!"

She was startled by a sharp ring at her own door bell. A moment later the maid appeared.

"A telegram for the master, Mrs. Dean," she said. "It came to the office, and Mr. Clark opened it, Joe says, thinking it was on business. But it wasn't, so he thought he'd better send it up to you, ma'am."

"Very well; thank you, Delia."

Louise took the envelope with its jagged edge showing where it had been hurriedly slit with the finger. Her heart leaped wildly at the first mention of a telegram, fearing it might be ill news of Gilbert. But no; there it was, addressed plainly, "Gilbert Dean," and she was so relieved that for an instant she forgot to draw out the inclosure. Then she recalled what Delia had said about its not being on business.

"In that case," she concluded, "it must be something in which I am interested."

She hastily threw aside the envelope, and read these words:

Will be in Albany tonight.   E. O.

"E. O." Louise repeated the letters musingly. "Who can that be? Why, I can't recall anybody Gilbert knows whose name begins with an O. 'E. O.'?" She closed her eyes for an instant as if to think the clearer, but the wrinkle did not leave her brow.

"I wonder if it is very important, if I ought to wire it on to him. But then he did not tell me where he was going to stop." This reflection came over her with a tinge of unpleasantness in it. She hated to think that even for one night her husband was beyond her call.

"He should have told me to what house he was going." She rested her elbow on the library table, on which the Albany Sunday paper still lay. Mechanically she ran her eye down the list of hotels, which happened to be just before her. Then suddenly a name in the adjoining column caught her attention. It was under the head of "Amusements," and was the announcement that "Borrowed Plumes" would be played in Albany Tuesday night. This was Tuesday night. Her glance shifted to the telegram again. "E. O." Estelle Osgood, the real name of Marie Myrwin, the actress, whom Gilbert had afterwards saved from the railroad wreck! But why should this woman send a telegram to him? Louise put the despatch down and pushed it away from her. She gave one quick glance about the room, to make sure she was alone. Her thoughts were so painfully intense; it seemed as though, were any one present, he must be able to read them.

Back over the intervening weeks her mind hurried, to the period, only a night it was, spent in that Western farmer's home. Surely there had been no opportunity there for Gilbert to become so well acquainted with the actress. Why, she even recalled chiding him for his indifference to her, he had behaved so oddly when in her presence.

But suddenly light was flashed upon the mystery from another quarter—Miss Myrwin's expression when told that it was Gilbert who had taken her from the wrecked car. "Did *he* save me?" she had exclaimed, and an expression of Louise knew not what nature had come into her eyes. She understood now; it was rapture, joy. What if she and Gilbert had known each other before?

And that night at the theater in Beverley! The note Gilbert had received! He said it was from a man, but now, as Louise looked back upon the circumstance in the light of this awful suspicion, it seemed unlikely that a man would send a note merely to call a friend outside. Why could he not come down and make the request in person? And Gilbert had been oddly abstracted on his return. Yes, and the next day on the train!

Proof was heaping up swiftly now, much too swiftly. Louise clasped both hands across her eyes as if to shut out some horrible vision. But this only made her see more clearly the firmly welded links in the chain of evidence that was bringing her to despair. She recollected Gilbert's restlessness after leaving Beverley. "And she was on board the train, and he told me he was going to look for a friend—a man. So Gilbert lied to me, and this is just what he did at the theater!" And she buried her face in her hands.

"But no," she exclaimed, raising her head suddenly. "No, I will not believe it. Gilbert has never deceived me. There must be some explanation. I will not allow myself to think about it any more. It is all so foolish."

But she could think of nothing else. She recalled how speedily Gilbert had returned from his search in the rear of the train, and then, on the plea of smoking, had gone forward—"into the smoking compartment," he had said, but she knew now it must have been into the forward coach, where this woman was.

"And he is in Albany with her now!" she murmured. She remembered his excuse—a favor for Illford. How carefully he had explained it all to her! He had not been in the habit of doing this. And she had thought his doing so in the present instance was only a new evidence of the depth of his regard for her! To his other sin was to be added hypocrisy. It was unbelievable—that all his attentions to her during the past few weeks, all his caresses, were hollow, mere blinds to conceal his defection!

"God of mercy," she murmured, "how can I bear it? What must I do?"

She recalled how she had discovered the actress' real name—seeing the initials E. O. on a watch which the Pullman conductor had found and brought to the farm house in search of an owner.

"I am Estelle Osgood," she had explained in identifying her property. "Myrwin is merely my stage name."

What if this incident had never happened, Louise asked herself? Was she grateful for the enlightenment it was afterwards to give her? Would ignorance be indeed bliss?

She rose and began to pace the floor; then, fearing that Delia might pass and see her thus strangely occupied, she walked to the window, and running up the shade, pressed her burning forehead against the cool pane. Upon the other side of the glass rain had begun to beat furiously; but if it were only this she had to face, she thought, how gladly would she go through it unprotected, in exchange for the mental anguish that was now her portion!

"And it was but a moment ago," she reflected, as her glance rested on the house across the street, "that I was pitying Mary Upton, contrasting her lot with my own! Her husband at least is sensible of his weakness, and makes an effort to master it. Mine—oh, heavens, his whole existence is a living lie!"

Her strength failed her; she sank down on a chair, misery and despair taking complete possession of her. How long would it be before others pitied her as she had pitied Mary Upton? People would stop talking when she came into the room that they might watch her unhampered; and then, when she had passed out again, how the whispered comments would hurry from tongue to ear, and how each would gaze after her compassionately, and wonder how she bore it at all!

There was a knock at the door.

"Oh!" Louise started up with a little scream. But it was only Delia, come to announce that dinner was served.

Louise went down and made a brave attempt to eat. The servants must not be allowed to suspect that anything was wrong. But it was torture to feel that they were watching her, and as soon as possible she returned up stairs and shut herself in the library again. Perhaps she need not keep up the deception long. The whole town might soon be aware of her husband's baseness.

She glanced at the clock on the mantel. It was nearly eight. But what difference did time make to her now? What had she to look forward to? Gilbert's return? Up to an hour ago she had been saying to herself, "This time tomorrow he will be back." Now his being with her would be torture worse than that she was already enduring. She would know that his every look, his every word, his every movement, in so far as they related to herself, were but a cruel mockery.

How should she receive him? She must outline some plan of action. The first emotion of humiliation, of mortification, having spent itself, anger began to obtrude. Her rights as a wife had been trampled on; she would not submit meekly. She would put him on the rack; would make him account to her for every second of his absence, and then, when he had rolled up a record of falsehoods that would rank well with those he had already told her, she would place the telegram in his hands, and tell him what she thought of him.

What would he say then, she wondered? What defense would he make, or would he attempt none? Suppose he threw himself upon her mercy, declared that he had been weak, but that now, seeing the enormity of his offense, he would turn from it and be the loving husband she had always supposed him? Would she forgive him then? Could she ever trust him again? Would there not always be a suspicion in her mind? The serpent had entered her paradise. Nothing now could be as it had been; her life was wrecked; her hopes, her ambitions, her pride—all had gone down beneath this blow, as some vessel might be going down even now before the pitiless storm that was rattling the windows and roaring down the chimney. But she must live on, nevertheless. Each day of her unhappiness would contain as many hours as those that went to make up her honeymoon; but each would seem thrice as long.

"And it was just after Gilbert had come back from talking with that woman on the train," she recollected now, with a shudder, "that I told him it seemed to me our honeymoon had never waned."

But she must not think of the past; there was a pang in every remembrance of it. How could she be sure that Gilbert had ever really loved her? She was conscious that outwardly she was not as attractive as many women. It was this fact, perhaps, that caused her to value her husband's affection so highly. And now that affection had turned to ashes in her grasp.

There was a tap at the door, and Delia appeared with a letter the postman had just brought. Louise took it listlessly. There was no longer zest for her in anything. When the maid had gone she walked to the mirror over the mantel. She was surprised that she saw so little alteration in the face that looked back at her. "But it will come," she murmured, "and people will talk low and say, 'Poor thing, how it has changed her!'"

Then she glanced down at the superscription on the envelope. "From Ethel," she murmured. "And she is coming here to visit next week. Shall I put her off?"

She returned to her chair, opened the letter and began to read. Presently a little ejaculation escaped her. "And now, my dear cousin," the letter ran, "I have a great surprise for you. I have just become engaged. He is the dearest boy—Malcolm Hunt. I have known him a year, but I feel as if it had been forever. I am sure I should not want to go away just now if I was not coming to you. I know you won't think me silly a bit when

I want to talk *him* all the time to you. You and Cousin Gilbert have always seemed to me different from other married people. It is just as if you weren't married—I mean, just as though you kept on being lovers, the way so many other people don't, after they are husband and wife."

Louise let the sheet fall. It was agony to read such words now. Her mind went back over the two years of her life with Gilbert. Had they been truly "lovers" all that while, as Ethel said? She knew that she had. And he—well, he had never spoken an unkind word to her, and if he had not been as free with his caresses as she with hers, she had set this down to his less demonstrative nature.

How would they deport themselves in the new life, which would begin as soon as he returned? It must differ from the old; it would be impossible for things to be as they had been. Ethel would not fail to notice the change. She must not be allowed to come. Louise would write to her, in the morning, that—yes, what would she write? She could not tell an untruth. That would be too much Gilbert's way. She caught her breath quickly at the comparison. But it was too true. Already she was beginning to despise him.

She finished the reading of the letter, and resolved to put off her decision till the morrow. Gilbert would be back then; she would talk it over with him.

The keenest pang of her ordeal shot through her as she realized what she was thinking. She had now none to whom to go for counsel. Her sole companion was her misery. She went to her room and hour after hour lay upon her bed, staring at the ceiling, at one moment trying to realize the full extent of her loneliness; at another seeking to deceive herself into the belief that this trouble had not really fallen upon her; that it was only part of some story which had made too deep an impression on her mind.

The November wind took up the rain and whirled it in fierce gusts against the windows. Louise imagined it to be her sorrow beating her down to the earth. Ah, it was cruel, to have deceived her so! If he had never loved her, why had he come to her at all with a pretense of doing so? For now that she was convinced of his infatuation for Estelle, she could not believe, she did not wish to believe, that he had ever really cared for her; did not want to feel that she had been put aside for this woman, an actress. Oh, it was too much! It was better never to have been loved; better to fancy that she had been deceived from the first. There would then at least not be the humiliation of believing he had grown tired of her.

But there was agony, too, in this other conviction, and no help to be found anywhere; and the morrow to be dreaded, and yet longed for, as there was no hope of sleep that night for such as she. And so, whether wished for or not, day dawned and brought no comfort to this wife who had discovered truth.

X.

ALTHOUGH the sky was weeping, and the bare branches of the trees lent a melancholy tinge to the November landscape, there was sunshine in Dean's heart as the train bore him swiftly toward the city where he would see Estelle again. No disturbing thought of Louise rose up to cloud his joyous anticipations. He had downed his conscience for the present at least. There would be time enough for a reckoning with it when his journey could be thought of only retrospectively.

The train reached Albany at half past five, and fifteen minutes later Dean was eagerly poring over the register at the Mohawk. His face lighted up as he discovered the name "Marie Myrwin," and in another instant his card was on its way to her room.

Estelle was dressing for dinner when the boy appeared with it. She shared the room with Sophie Waters, the soubrette. Sophie was out of humor because she hadn't received a letter which she expected to find awaiting her. Estelle was despondent. This was nothing new; but tonight she was feeling more than ordinarily depressed. She was thinking that she had had but the word to say and the man who filled her heart would have come to her, would perhaps be with her now. Albany was only four hours distant from Islington. The company would probably never be any closer to the town which now, to her eyes, stood out from the map as if printed in letters of a different color.

"If I had only sent the despatch sooner," she was thinking, "he would have come. But I knew this, and sent it purposely too late. It was right for me to do so; his wife was very kind to me, but oh, heavens, so was he. He saved my life, and I love him, I love him!"

It was at this point the boy with the card knocked. When Estelle opened the door and learned who had asked for her, she could scarcely repress a little cry of joy. There was no thought of denying him. "Tell him I will be down at once," she told the boy.

And when they met in the quiet parlor of this quiet house, there was another greeting such as a husband would give a wife, and for a while each forgot that the joy was a stolen one; or if they remembered, the thought only added a sweeter taste to it. Then Estelle shook her finger reprovingly at Dean.

"I thought I told you that you were not to see me any more," she said; "and you promised."

"But that was when I believed you were going to be beyond my reach. I can't starve my heart all the time. One look into your eyes, one touch of your hand, are reward for all that I may have to undergo to obtain them."

"Then this is the last. We shall not be in Albany again."

"Yes, the last, Estelle, if you will be very good to me this time. So you see it depends on yourself. Now will you come out to dinner with me, and then let me take you to the theater?"

"On those conditions, yes, Gilbert."

She was soon ready, and they were out in the rain soaked street. But the elements counted for little with these two. For each, just now, nothing existed but the other. Each saw the love light in the other's eyes as they sat at the table in the cozy corner of the restaurant, and each resolutely put away all thoughts of the morrow. When they were in the cab on the way to the theater Dean said suddenly, "Tell me something, Estelle. You say you did not know I was married when you sent for me that night in Beverley. What if—what if I had not been, and I had asked you to be my wife, what would you have said?"

"My heart would have said yes, dear, but my sense of duty no. I am no longer in the circle to which once we both belonged. I am a woman of the stage. It would only drag you down to marry me; it is dragging you down to be with me now."

"You must not talk that way, Estelle.

There is no purer being on earth than you. I could do anything, be anything, that you bade, and doing it, being it, be the better man, for you would not demand that which was not right. If I were only free——"

"Don't, Gilbert; now it is my turn to beg you not to speak in that way. You are not free; your duty is to your wife, who was once so kind to me, and yet from whom, Heaven forgive me, I shrank, because she was that to you I could never be."

Dean left Estelle at the stage door, then went round to the box office and bought a seat for himself close to the footlights.

During the time that Estelle was on the stage, he sat there entranced. How graceful were all her movements, how soft and flexible her voice, and in her beauty she was peerless. His heart beat fast. She caught his eye and smiled at him. His soul was on fire. When she appeared on the stage again a little later, she had a love scene with Harry Vane, and Dean became horribly jealous. It seemed to him that the actor held Estelle in his arms a great deal longer than was necessary, and every caress was a dagger thrust to Gilbert.

When the play was over he met Estelle and took her to supper. They lingered at the table till past midnight, and Dean wondered how he was ever going to endure the old life to which he must return—the life that was a lie.

And Estelle—she looked at this man who she knew loved her with all his heart, whom she loved more devotedly than ever since he had risked his own life to save hers, and a fierce rebellion took possession of her. Why must she give him up? He really belonged to her. No other woman could love him as she loved him, and was not love like hers stronger than marriage vows? Should not this attraction of heart to heart be kept sacred and held in deference? It was against nature that Gilbert Dean should belong to Louise Dartmouth and not to Estelle Osgood. Louise might love him deeply, but did he love her? No. Then there was no reciprocity, and by every prompting of humanity, Estelle's claim should be recognized.

At least such were the wild arguments that went surging through the actress' brain as she began counting the minutes before they must part. What if she should speak some of them to Dean? Suppose he shared her views, but had hesitated about expressing himself? If he offered to give up wife, home, his brilliant future, all for her, would she have the strength to resist, as she had told him a few hours before that duty would have prompted her to resist him had he asked her to be his wife that night in Beverley?

For an instant she gave her imagination the reins, and saw herself and Gilbert flying from duty, from the right, abandoned to love, with no other thought than to be happy. And would they be? Ah, no. A shiver passed over her. Dean noticed it.

"What is it, Estelle?" he asked anxiously, tenderly.

"I was only thinking—thinking how wrong it is for you to be here, how wrong in me to have let you come."

"But you didn't let me come," he answered,

with a smile. "I came on the mere chance that I would find you here. Call it chance that I came."

"I can't, Gilbert. I was weak. I might have telegraphed sooner and told you—well, told you we were not to play here. A written lie would have been better than the acted one you have been living tonight."

"Telegraphed sooner, Estelle!" he replied. "What did you mean by that? You did not telegraph at all."

"Ah, but I did; sent the message when I knew it would be too late for you to catch the train to bring you here."

A wrinkle creased Dean's forehead.

"You did telegraph me, Estelle?" he exclaimed. "For heaven's sake, what did you say in the message?"

"Why, Gilbert, did I do anything wrong? You asked me to wire you when we were to play in Albany."

"But I did not suppose any such message would come after I had left. Quick, what did you say?"

"Let me think. Oh, my dear, I hope I have not been the means of bringing trouble to you!"

"No, it is probably all right." Dean caught his breath quickly between each word. "Only tell me just what you said, if you can remember."

"I think it was this: 'Will be in Albany tonight.'"

"And what did you sign it?"

Dean leaned forward eagerly for the answer.

"Why, just simply 'E. O.' But you look very serious. Was it wrong? You told me to telegraph, you know."

"You sent it to the office, did you not?" said Dean, his hand trembling slightly.

"Yes; just where I have addressed the letters," Estelle replied. "Tell me, do you think any harm has come of it? If there has——"

"Don't worry, Estelle." But his face was a shade whiter. "It is probably all right. You did just as I told you, any way. Do not let us spoil our last few minutes together by being anxious over mere possibilities."

But the shadow did not lift from Estelle's face. As they walked back to the hotel—for the rain had ceased at midnight—she kept continually reverting to the matter. "I knew I was right, Gilbert," she said, "when I told you that day on the train that you ought not to see me again. It means danger for both of us. You will let me know, dear, will you not, whether—whether any evil has befallen by reason of that despatch?"

"Surely I will, little one. Don't forget to give me your route before I leave you."

"Only till Friday; that will be long enough for news of today to reach me. After that you must not write again."

Dean did not plead; he knew that Estelle would relent.

"Tell me that you love me, dear," he said instead; "that you will think of me every day, and won't forget your promise to let me know if you are in trouble."

They were near the hotel now. There was no one else in the street. She looked up into his face in the starlight.

"I do love you with all my heart, Gilbert; love you too well to permit any harm to come to you through me."

"And by one foolish act I put myself beyond such love. Oh, Heaven be kind to me!" The words were uttered with a dramatic effect finer than anything Estelle had ever played to on the stage. The pathos of it swept away all reserve. She put out her hands to him. He drew her into his arms, and the kiss she gave him was as manna to his starving soul.

"Why must I not see her again?" he asked himself after he had gone to his room. "If that telegram has betrayed me, I might as well be betrayed for much as for little."

The company were to play in Newark the next day, and before he slept Dean wrote this note to Estelle:

> I shall take breakfast with you at eight. I have decided to accompany you as far as Poughkeepsie. I can then just make the connections that will get me back in Islington by nine in the evening.

Estelle rebuked him with her lips when he met her the next morning, but there was joy in her eyes. He took a chair next to hers in the drawing room car, and once more they talked of the old days in Lakefield, and the morning flew by on the wings of love. Once Dean heard a little girl across the aisle whisper, "Mama, don't you think they are bride and groom?" He smiled when he repeated this to Estelle, but she looked grave as she replied:

"What if she knew the truth?"

When Dean left her at Poughkeepsie, he stood on the platform of the station and watched a fluttering handkerchief at one of the car windows of the New York train till she who held it was carried beyond his vision. Then he heaved a great sigh, and turned his face back towards Islington.

XI.

IF the night had seemed long to Louise, the day succeeding it appeared endless. And yet, when she thought of what the future might have in store, she felt that she ought to cling covetously to every minute of the present, fraught with anguish as it was. The sun shone brilliantly after the storm, and the flood of light that poured in at the windows was such a mockery of the gloom that enshrouded her soul that she wished the rain might have continued.

She had an engagement at eleven to go to the hospital and read for an hour to a patient whom her circle of King's Daughters had taken in charge. It was a woman whose husband had left her, and who was dying of a broken heart. Louise pictured her own friends talking afterwards of how it must have tried her soul to minister to one whose trouble was so closely akin to her own. She did not see how she could go today, but she knew it was her duty; and only duty was left to her now.

When afternoon came she shut herself in her room on the pretense of sleeping, but really to think, to plan. Should she tell Gilbert of her discovery? She carried that telegram in the bosom of her gown. Yes, she must tell him of it. The message belonged to him; she had no right to keep it after he arrived.

Suppose he should admit his guilt, what must then be her course? Her inclination would be to go away somewhere, where she would never see him again, never hear his name; but that would be equivalent to publishing his disgrace to the world, providing it were not known already.

What if this were the case, and she were the last instead of the first to know of her husband's defection? Could this possibly be— that she had been pitied and talked about, and blamed, perhaps? But whether this were so or not, where could she go? She was now living in the home that had been hers from a child. Her parents were both dead. She remembered how people said, when her father died, what a fortunate thing it was she had married such a sterling fellow as Gilbert Dean, who could take Mr. Dartmouth's place in everything that went to the management of the great business and the making of the luxurious home.

There was Uncle John Peterson, who lived on a farm over in Vermont. She would see no one if she went there, and he was true as steel, and would care for her devotedly. But what would life be worth to a woman of her tastes and aspirations, buried away from all culture and social contact with the busy world of thought and action?

No, she would not submit to being driven out from that which was really her own. If any one was to go, it must be he, who had brought this shadow upon her life. She had done no wrong; he was guilty, and must suffer. And it was in this mood that she passed the day.

While she was at dinner a telegram came from Dean, dated in Albany, saying he would be home at nine. Louise checked the sensation of joy that possessed her at the thought of soon seeing him again. "He is not worthy of my respect even," she told herself. "Why must I give him my love? He has made me suffer. Now it will be his turn."

As nine o'clock drew near, a feverish excitement began to possess her. She felt her cheeks to be burning. She tried to arrange in her mind just the order in which she would convict him out of his own mouth. She would not spare. Why should she? He had not spared her. That he meant to keep her in ignorance of his offense against her, counted for nothing. How two faced he had been! What a hypocrite he was! No wonder he had risked his life to rescue this woman, this actress! And she, Louise, had called him brave for doing it, and had tenderly cared for the woman, held her in her arms, stroked the hair back from her temples, watched beside her bed! Oh, it was monstrous that such things could be; it was a miracle that Gilbert could look her in the face, could take——

Ah, there was his key in the lock now! Her first impulse was not to go to meet him, as she ordinarily did. But that would awaken suspicion. She did not wish to do this; she must show more diplomacy. She would convince him that there were actresses as clever as those who trod the boards of the theater. Then she hurried out into the hall and flung her arms about his neck with all her old time fervor. She wondered a little that she did not shrink from the contact, but she was watching herself closely.

"Did you get my telegram?" he asked, as, with his arm about her waist, he returned with her to the library, where his easy chair was ready for him in front of the burning logs in the grate.

"Yes, while I was at dinner. It was so thoughtful of you to wire me. But then, that is just like you, Gilbert; always thinking to do little things that will please me." She watched to note if he would flinch on hearing this, but not a muscle quivered; at least not so long as she dared look. She found that she could not entirely trust herself yet.

He sank into his chair with a sigh of content. "How good it is to be at home again," he murmured; and putting out his hand, he drew her to a favorite seat—on an ottoman beside him, where she could rest both arms across his knee and look up into his face.

"You have missed me, then, Gilbert?" she asked softly.

"Of course I have missed you, little one. You want me to tell you how often your face kept coming between me and those prosy legislators I was trying to move in Illford's behalf?" He bent down and kissed her again.

"And did you succeed? Do you think you will get the bill through?" She could scarcely steady her voice sufficiently to frame the words. She was thinking of the traitorous embrace she had just received; of the awful string of falsehoods she had now opened the way for him to tell.

"I think we shall," he replied, without an instant's hesitation. "I put in some good work this morning. I couldn't do as much as I expected last night."

"What did you do with yourself last evening, then? Didn't it rain in Albany.

"Yes, poured. Illford and I sat in the lobby of the hotel, smoking and swapping stories of frontier life. You know he was in the army once; was quartered at Fort Niobrara. He was quite surprised to hear that I had been for six months on a Texan ranch. Do you remember what a cowboy guy I was when you first saw me there, Louise?"

"You were never a guy in my eyes, Gilbert," she replied quickly. She forgot, for the instant, the hated task she had set herself. She was transported in memory back to that night when her heart told her that her eyes were looking upon a man she could easily love. But it was only an instant's lapse; sweeping over her again came the consciousness of the full perfidy of her husband, who could so easily pile untruth upon untruth. She must test him still further, and then reveal what she knew.

She reached out one hand and took that Sunday paper from the table.

"So you stayed at the hotel all the evening," she went on, glancing with apparent carelessness up and down the columns. "I rather thought you might go to the theater."

"To the theater?" he replied, in well affected surprise. "Why, my dear, you know that you care more for that sort of thing than I do."

"But I thought the attraction in this instance," she went on, with a tinge of sarcasm, "would be too strong for you to resist. The 'Borrowed Plumes' company was playing in Albany last night. Surely you have not forgotten Estelle Osgood?" She held the paper up for him to see, with her finger on the announcement. But her eyes were fixed on his face.

There was only surprise in his. "Why, is that so?" he exclaimed, taking the paper. "It is too bad I did not know of it. I might have taken Illford. I could have told him the story of that experience of ours with the leading woman, and he would have been doubly interested."

Louise's lip was trembling by this time. What an accomplished liar her husband was! She inserted one hand in her corsage and drew out the telegram. "If this had not come too late," she said, rising as she passed it over to him, "you would have had no excuse for not knowing."

She stepped back to the mantelpiece, rested one elbow upon it, and watched him as he read the despatch. It seemed but an instant that he glanced at it, then he had crushed it together in his hand, and had come over to stand in front of her.

"What do you mean, Louise?" he asked. There was no terror in his tones, no sign of nervousness even. "What has this telegram to do with Miss Osgood?"

"Everything, as it is from her. No, don't speak. You already have enough to answer for, and now that I have found you out, you need no longer wear the mask. So you went to Albany to oblige Mr. Illford, and stayed with him at the hotel all the evening, smoking and telling stories! And I—I was sitting here alone with that message before me, its every word burning into my soul the conviction of your treachery. I would not believe it at first, but with the proof in my hand, oh, merciful Heaven, what else could I do?"

She felt that her voice was breaking; that tears of anguish were forcing themselves to her eyes, which she had hoped, instead, to make blaze with indignation. She turned away and bowed her head upon the mantel. She figured herself remembering this culminating moment in her life's history to her dying day: the moment when Gilbert knew that she knew his deception.

"And on such slight evidence as this you believe so much ill of me." He was speaking softly into her ear; she could just feel his arm as he passed it lightly around her.

She faced him quickly. "Prove that I was wrong," she entreated. "But you cannot, you cannot. Those were her initials; you knew her before that accident, I am sure you did; and you went to Albany expressly to meet her. How could you so deceive me?"

"You have jumped at conclusions, woman like, Louise." Dean's voice was as firm as it had ever been in his life. It was one of the times when it had to be firm. "Listen: this message is from Illford. He told me he had sent it, thinking he had not made it quite plain in his letter just when he would be in Albany, as he had two dates under consideration."

"But how could it be from Mr. Illford?" Louise interposed. "His initials are not E. O."

"No, but they are E. I.—Eugene Illford. The mistake is easily accounted for. In telegraphy two dots stand for both letters, but there is a little longer space between them in the O than in the I. The operator simply did not pay close enough attention, and got them mixed. Why, my dear little girl, you don't know how it pains me to have you think such monstrous things of me. Besides, consider how absurd your supposition was. When did this telegram arrive?"

"It was sent up here from the office about half past five yesterday afternoon."

"Well, then, granting it was from Miss Osgood, of what use would it have been to me, as I could not possibly get to Albany that night, and the company, as you can see for yourself by the paper, play there for that date only."

"But the same reason would show that the despatch was not sent by Mr. Illford," Louise responded.

"With this difference," Dean answered at once; "that he expected to stop over today as he did, and only sent this message as an extra measure of precaution, to insure my being there some time during his stay. Are you satisfied now, little one?"

Louise threw her head back and looked up into his face. How she longed to believe him, to trust him! And why should she not? Was not his story a reasonable one? As she regarded it now, with this new light cast upon it, the light of love, how flimsy a structure seemed that fabric of deceit she had brought herself to look upon as her husband's work! Placed beneath the rays of this powerful illuminant, even that episode in the farm house dwindled into insignificance. There were a hundred ways of accounting for that woman's strange words on being told who had been her rescuer other than the one her suspicions had caused her to hit upon. And as for the incident in the theater at Beverley, and on the train, why, the sting she had found in these was altogether of her own making. Was not she the unworthy one? Their eyes met; his did not waver. "Gilbert, my husband, forgive me!" she cried, throwing her arms about his neck.

She clung there, weeping convulsively. How cruelly she had wronged him! She did not deserve such generous treatment at his hands.

"I am not worthy of you, Gilbert," she sobbed.

Louise was radiantly happy now, so happy, indeed, that presently she began to make light of her misery.

"Why, I even envied poor Mrs. Upton," she said. "And I was wondering where I should go if it came to my leaving you. But it was very lucky the occasion didn't arise, because I knew I should be miserable in any place without you. And once I actually caught myself planning to wait and ask your advice. Fancy that, when I imagined that you had gone off and left me! Wasn't it absurd?" And Louise laughed, and Dean laughed with her, and then she became almost hysterical as she recalled how confidently she had expected never to see his lips part in a smile for her again.

"This is the happiest day of my life, dear," she said to him as they went up stairs together.

"And of mine," he whispered back. And he wondered why a bolt from heaven did not strike him dead for the lie; and when Louise had gone to her dressing room he stood for a moment at the window, looking up at the stars, and doubting if they shone down on a more wretched man in all the world.

XII.

THE days following Gilbert's return from Albany were joyous ones to Louise. Despising herself for her unjust suspicions, she was constantly discovering new evidences of her husband's affection. For Dean was careful now to be liberal in bestowing these. But in spite of that one night's contrition, his heart was still in Estelle's keeping. He had written to her the next morning, telling her not to distress herself about that telegram, for no harm had resulted. And she had replied, and thus the correspondence went on as briskly as before.

These letters from Dean were Estelle's most valued treasures. She looked upon them as the last link connecting her with the old life, that life where women were always respected, and no coarseness of speech was ever suffered to come within their hearing. Her present environment had been sufficiently irksome before that night when the company played in Beverley. But then she had only become weary of it at times; now it was continually hateful to her. Yet she saw no escape; she was absolutely dependent on her salary, every penny of which must be carefully guarded lest she might not have enough to carry her through the long summer vacation. Relatives she had none, except those that were poorer than herself, and they had cast her off since she had gone on the stage.

Her present companions were friendly enough; too friendly at times. Harry Vane's attentions were odious to her. He had a wife traveling with another company. Estelle's soul sickened within her when she was driven to remind him of this fact, and he replied, "Well, my dear, I accord her the privilege of consoling herself as I am trying to do."

Contrasted with men such as these, Gilbert Dean seemed godlike, weak as Estelle recognized him to be. But then that weakness was betrayed only in yielding to his regard for her; and a woman can easily forgive such a failing in a man. His love, hopeless as she knew it to be, was the one thing that now made life worth living. It would be like stilling her very heart beats to put it out of her soul, and so she did not try. Although the thought was never formulated into an expectation, she knew that some time, somewhere, and soon, she would see Dean again. And Dean shared this hope—or rather not hope; with him it was an intention.

So the winter passed, and when spring came Estelle wrote that early in May the company were to play a one night stand in Islington. The local opera house had been renovated, and had been offered on such favorable terms to manager Roberts, that he had decided to cancel one date in Syracuse. Dean scarcely knew whether he was more rejoiced or disturbed to receive these tidings. To know that Estelle would be in the same town, and to be unable to be with her, would be unendurable; and yet, here, at home, how could he manage it without betraying himself? But that he would manage it by some means, at whatever risk, he knew perfectly well.

As the day drew near, a feverish impatience seized him; and then, on the very morning when the "Borrowed Plumes" posters were put up in town, Illford appeared. Dean was out when he called at the office, but he found his card on his return, "Sorry to miss you. Will be busy the rest of the day, but will drop in on you at your home tonight."

Dean stood staring at the bit of pasteboard as though it were endowed with the ability to inflict bodily injury on him. What should he do? Louise must not meet this man. Oh, of course there was no likelihood that she would. How absurd to be so fearful! A smile, but a faint one, curled the corner of his mustache, as he crushed the card together and dropped it into his overcoat pocket. It was not necessary that Louise should meet his business friends who called at the house to see him, although, to be sure she often did. It would be safer to send Illford word not to come; to say that he would not be at home.

But Dean did not know where to send the message. There was positively no way of communicating with the man.

"Then I must take Louise and go out somewhere tonight," Dean decided, and he began to cast about in his mind for a place to go. And as he thought, he grew calmer. He remembered how skilfully he had extricated himself from the telegram dilemma; surely his wits would not fail him now.

"Louise," he said, when he went home that night, "don't you want to go around with me to the Nevilles' this evening?" And she, delighted to go anywhere with her husband, gladly acquiesced.

"Let us start early, dear," he added, "so that we can come home in good time." He was fearful least Illford might call before they got off.

He had his hat on, and was holding the front door open for his wife to pass out, when she exclaimed, "Oh, Gilbert, I snatched up my gloves so hastily that they are both for the same hand. Please go get the right one for me."

"How very stupid," he muttered, as he hurried off to do her bidding.

Louise looked after him wonderingly. It was not like Gilbert to talk in this way. There was a step on the graveled driveway. An instant later a figure appeared at the door.

"Is Mr. Dean at home?" the newcomer asked.

It was a man whom Louise did not know— a gentleman, she saw at a glance.

"Yes," she replied. "That is, we were just going out. Won't you walk in? My husband will be down stairs in a moment."

"He had a previous engagement, then. I am sorry, but I will wait and speak to him."

"Oh, no, it was no regular engagement," Louise returned pleasantly. "We were merely going out to call on some friends. Gilbert— Mr. Dean—suggested it while we were at dinner."

"Then he could not have received my card— but here he is, to speak for himself," and Illford walked toward the stairway, meeting Dean at the foot of it.

"Why, my dear fellow," the master of the house exclaimed, "this *is* a surprise. When did you arrive in town?"

"This morning. I dropped in on you at your office, but you were out, so I scribbled a message on a card and left it on your desk. Did you not see it?"

"Not a sign of it. Must have blown out of the window; things sometimes do. What did you say on it? But come on up to the library, and we'll have a smoke. Louise, you will excuse me, I know."

"Certainly, my dear." She had come to the stairway, expecting that her husband would introduce his friend, but he made no motion to do so, and the two went off up stairs together.

Louise strolled into the drawing room, and with her wraps still about her sat there for some time, thoughtfully turning her wedding ring round and round upon her finger. There had been something strange about Gilbert ever since he came home tonight. She recalled now that he had been unwontedly silent at the table until he had suddenly proposed making this call on the Nevilles, which was in itself an odd thing for him to do. Then he had hurried her off, was cross because she had brought the wrong glove, and now he had been almost rude in not introducing her. He must have heard her talking with his caller as he came down stairs.

"I think I will give him a little scolding," she decided, "after his friend has gone. If it is a business worry, he ought not to bring it home with him, or else he should tell me all about it, and let me help him bear it."

She rose, and started to go up to her own room, to lay aside her things. In crossing the hall her glance chanced to fall on something white lying on the floor just outside the coat closet. She could hear a low murmur of voices in the library up stairs. Gilbert must have closed the door, for no odor of cigar smoke came down to her. She stooped to pick up the crumpled card and toss it into the waste paper basket, when penciled writing on it caught her eye.

"It is something Gilbert has dropped from his overcoat pocket in taking out his gloves," she thought.

She smoothed out the bit of pasteboard, and read these words: "Sorry to miss you. Will be busy the rest of the day, but will call on you at your house tonight."

Louise quickly turned the card, and saw the name—

> EUGENE ILLFORD.

She was not prepared for this. She put out her hand as if to clutch the empty air for support, and then sank weakly into the little cushioned recess that made a cozy seat by the fireplace. In swift panorama all her husband's strange actions of the evening marshaled themselves before her mental vision. Each one pointed to the same conclusion: he did not wish her to see this man, the man to meet whom he had told her he had gone to Albany last fall.

And that woman, that actress, was coming

to Islington. Louise recalled noticing the posters of the play around the streets that very afternoon. This man Illford doubtless knew just what Gilbert had done on that trip to Albany. Merciful heavens, must that fearful chapter in her wifehood be lived over again? Had her husband added a new series of hypocrisies to his yet deeper crime, and were all the tokens of affections he had lavished upon her since that memorable November night, but so many blinds to cover up his perfidy?

The first sharp pang passed, Louise began to shape her course of action. She could do this with more coolness than on that previous occasion. Then, the horror of it all was too fresh to permit her to think with any degree of coolness. Now, although her heart was bleeding, she compelled her head to assume control.

Retaining the card, she went up to her own room, and sat there, with her wraps on, till she heard her husband's visitor depart. Then she came out and met Gilbert on the stairs. "Is it too late to go to the Nevilles' now, my dear?" she asked.

She noted that Gilbert was nervous; she could detect that he was watching her, seeking to try to inform himself whether any suspicion had been awakened in her mind.

"Yes, I am afraid it is too late, my love," he answered her, looking at his watch. "That bore of a Brooks would stay on. He is always making his appearance at the wrong times, and never going at the right ones."

Louise's heart had given a quick bound when Gilbert mentioned his friend as Brooks. Perhaps she was mistaken after all, and that card of Illford's had no connection with the man who had called. But she would keep it and find out, if she had to go down to the office and question the clerks as to the appearance of the man who had left it.

"I thought it a little odd you didn't introduce him, Gilbert," was all she said now. "You must have heard me talking to him."

"He is not the man I would want my wife to know, Louise," was Dean's reply. She was looking steadily at him, and noted the telltale flush that dyed his cheeks.

Before they retired that night, Gilbert announced that he must breakfast early and drive on business to Raymond Falls.

"Perhaps I will show him that card to-night," Louise said to herself the next morning, as she stood on the piazza for a moment after she had bidden him good by.

At this instant a figure turned in at the gateway, and Louise beheld the caller of the night previous advancing up the drive. Her heart began to beat faster as she realized the opportunity for undisturbed investigation that was now presented to her. She moved toward the steps to meet this early morning visitor.

He raised his hat as he came up. "Is Mr. Dean at home?" he asked.

"No," answered Louise. "My husband has just started on a drive to Raymond Falls."

"I am sorry to miss him. I thought I would catch him before he went to his office."

"You can find him there later in the day. He will be back by ten."

"But I leave town on the eight thirty train. I am Mr. Illford."

"Oh!" The exclamation uttered by Louise was almost a gasp.

"I wished to see Mr. Dean for a few minutes about a matter I forgot to speak of last night."

Louise was greatly excited, but she exerted all her self control and remained outwardly calm. "Won't you walk up and take a seat, Mr. Illford?" she said. "It is not yet time for your train."

"Thank you;" and he followed her to a shaded corner of the piazza.

"Perhaps you would like to leave a message with me," she added, as they seated themselves. "I have often heard my husband speak of you, Mr. Illford."

"Yes?"

"It was you he went to meet in Albany last November, I believe—one of the very few trips he has ever taken without me."

"Meet me in Albany?" exclaimed Illford, in perplexity.

"Why, yes; don't you remember the occasion? It had something to do with a bill of yours before the Legislature."

"A bill of mine before the Legislature?" Illford repeated, still puzzled.

"Perhaps it wasn't called a bill, then." Louise forced a little laugh. "You know we women are always stupid where anything connected with politics is concerned, except when we are strong minded. At any rate, you and he were there together, on some affair of importance."

"But really you mystify me, Mrs. Dean. I have never had anything to do with legislative business, and I have not been to Albany in two years. You must be confusing me with some other friend of your husband."

"Possibly I am." Louise wondered how she possessed the strength to frame the words. The world appeared to be reeling away from her. Her worst suspicions were confirmed. Gilbert had lied to her. But she must not give way now. "You said something about a message," she went on, oblivious of the fact that it was she herself who had spoken of this. "Won't you leave it with me? That is, if it is not of too abstruse a business character."

Illford thought he had never seen a sadder smile on a human face. He recalled this fact vividly afterwards.

"Oh, I need not trouble you with one, Mrs. Dean," he replied. "I can write after I reach home. And now I must be going, or I shall miss my train. Good morning. Say to Mr. Dean that I am very sorry I missed him."

Louise rose as her caller passed her on his way to the steps. She placed one hand firmly against a pillar of the porch, and leaned heavily against it.

"Good morning, Mr. Illford," she forced herself to say. "I will tell my husband you were here." Then, as her caller's back was turned, she set her lips tightly together, and a firm resolve entered her soul.

XIII.

IT was late in the afternoon of the same day. The Dean carriage stood before the gate, and, card case in hand, Louise came forth and entered it. "Drive down to the Tremley House, David," she said to the coachman.

The faithful old Scotchman was rather surprised at this order. His mistress was not in the habit of calling at this hotel, the principal one in the town though it was. He was more amazed than ever, however, when, after a brief halt at the Tremley, Mrs. Dean returned to the carriage with the order, " Drive around to the Forest King."

This was the other hotel in the town, of not quite such high standing as the Tremley, much frequented by commercial travelers, and the few theatrical companies that took in Islington on their routes.

"The missus must be on a quare charity errand this day, and no mistake," David soliloquized, as he drew up before the ladies' entrance to the rather dingy hostelry with the pretentious name.

There was no attendant at the side door, and Louise was obliged to wait until the clerk in the office caught a glimpse of her, and sent a shambling bell boy to learn her wishes.

"Is Miss Myrwin stopping here?"

"Do you mean the actress lady?" asked the bell boy.

"Yes," said Louise. "Will you take up this card to her?"

The boy took the card and went off with it. Louise found the door of the reception room, and sank down on the sofa. But her lips were firmly set still; she had made up her mind to accomplish a certain purpose, and was determined not to flinch because it might be disagreeable to carry out. "If she is not in I will come again," she told herself.

But Estelle was in. The boy came back in the course of a few minutes with word that the caller was to walk up to the parlor on the next floor. Louise wondered, as she took her way thither, whether the boy would tell the clerk who she was, and thus start bar room comment on the strangeness of her visit.

Estelle appeared in the doorway of the dingy drawing room a few minutes after she herself had arrived there. "Why, Mrs. Dean," she exclaimed, "how good of you to come!"

It was with an effort that Louise took the hand held out to her. It lay as a piece of ice in her own hand, but the actress' cheeks were flaming.

"I wanted to know how you were," Louise replied. "I shall not soon forgot the day we passed together in that Nebraska farmer's home."

"When you were so very, very kind to me." Estelle dropped her eyes from her caller's persistent gaze as she murmured the words.

"Have you entirely recovered from the shock of the accident?" Louise went on, asking herself if the interview could possibly be inflicting as much torture on this other woman as it was on herself.

"Oh, yes, indeed; long, long ago. You were such a capital nurse, Mrs. Dean. I wish that I might repay you in some way for what you did for me, an utter stranger."

"I could not have done less, Miss Osgood." Estelle instinctively shrank away a little at the coldness of this response. "You were within a few hours of us in the fall, I believe," Louise continued after an instant.

"We played one night in Albany," Estelle answered in a very low tone.

"Yes, Mr. Dean was in Albany that same night." There was something in Louise's voice that sent a thrill to Estelle's soul. How much did Gilbert's wife know, she asked herself? A deadly fear took possession of her. She had foreboded ill when she learned who had called. Now she felt that the supreme moment had come. The eyes of this woman were fixed on her face as though they would read her through and through.

"Did you not see him?" Estelle heard this

question as in a dream. How should she answer? She recalled Gilbert's reassuring letter; that it was all right about that telegram; that she need not worry.

"Yes," she admitted waveringly.

"You are franker than my husband," rejoined Louise, in a voice of steel. "He did not mention the fact to me."

The agony that was now depicted on Estelle's face would have been pitiful to a less merciless observer. She knew not what to say; it seemed to her as if the end of all things had come.

"Perhaps, then, you can tell me——" Louise started to continue, when the bell boy entered the room.

"A gentleman to see you, Miss Myrwin," he said, and he handed Estelle a card.

Louise was white. She knew intuitively that it was her husband's card, and now, as Estelle took it from the salver, she was sure of it, from its peculiar shape.

An expression of consternation came into the eyes of the actress. "Tell him," she stammered, and then paused, her confusion overwhelming her. "Tell him," she began again—"tell him I cannot see him."

"Tell him she *will* see him," interposed Louise, in commanding tones.

The earnestness of her words compelled the boy to obey. Estelle raised her hand in protest, and called hysterically after him; but once safely out of the room he had no thought of returning.

"The presence of his wife should not deprive Mr. Dean of the pleasure of seeing you," said Louise, in contemptuous irony. Her words cut deep, but Estelle made no reply. She was dazed. What would another minute bring forth?

For six months Dean had not seen the woman who filled his heart to the exclusion of all others. He burst into the room with eager joy. He had almost reached Estelle, his hands outstretched, when he stopped, stunned—there was his wife!

It was an awful moment. He staggered back, as one thrust through by a dagger. His brain reeled; his wife's eyes burned into his very soul. He tried to speak. Louise raised her hand.

"An unexpected pleasure for you, Mr. Dean, no doubt," she said, with biting sarcasm. "You could hardly have anticipated finding your wife with this woman."

Estelle sprang to her feet with flashing eyes. "You have no right, madam, to refer to me in such words."

"I have the right to say what I choose to this man; I was not addressing you."

Louise had the stronger nature. Estelle felt this—realized the feebleness of her protest. Louise went on.

"I have trapped you at last," she said, turning again to her husband; "trapped you in her very presence. Your infamy is plain to me now. I have seen Illford, and know all. He was not in Albany last November. You did not go there to meet him, but to be with this woman—your companion in shame."

Dean took a quick step forward. The honor of her he loved had been assailed. It mattered not that the assailant was his wife. "I will not permit you to imply aught against Miss Osgood," he cried hotly.

Louise answered with a bitter sneer.

"I take my oath that she is as pure as yourself," Dean went on, now thoroughly aroused.

"*Your* oath, Gilbert Dean," exclaimed Louise, with ineffable scorn. "The oath of a man who can perjure himself as you have done!" Her voice was raised; her face was white with righteous wrath. "I have done with you forever," she cried. "You will have to cover up your infidelity with no more falsehoods. She can have you, miserable woman!" And Louise started to leave the room.

Dean sprang forward and caught her by the wrist. "You shall not go like this," he commanded. "You must believe me; I have told you the truth. You are mad, Louise. For God's sake, think what you have said!"

"Coward!" she muttered, and, wrenching herself from his grasp, fled from the room and out past the listeners who had gathered in the hall.

XIV.

SEVEN o'clock the next morning. The waitress at the Deans' has just entered the dining room to throw open the shutters and make ready for breakfast. She has let in the cheerful sunlight from three of the windows. In starting toward the fourth, she sees something at her feet, almost trips over it, in fact. It is the prostrate figure of a woman—Mrs. Dean. The eyes are staring, looking up at the terrified servant with a glassiness that can mean but one thing.

The girl drops to her knees and places a hand against the white cheek. It is ice cold. She springs up and flies shrieking from the room. The other servants rush forth, but the waitress can tell them only that their mistress is lying dead upon the floor. Then she runs up the stairway, calling out "Mr. Dean, Mr. Dean!" while the coachman goes for the doctor.

But Mr. Dean is not to be found. The room which he usually occupies with his wife is empty; the bed has not been disturbed. In the mean time the physician has arrived.

"It is too late," were his first words. "Poor Mrs. Dean!" he added. "What can this mean?"

A closer examination revealed marks about the throat that suggested a tragedy.

"This must be the explanation," reasoned the doctor; "but who could have committed this horrible crime? Gilbert? Oh, no, no—it can't be, and yet he is missing."

Quickly the news flies from tongue to tongue; quickly it spreads over the town; quickly it flashes along the wires to the metropolis, and the eyes of the world are turned toward the scene of the tragedy. Islington itself is stirred to fever heat. The wildest rumors gain credence, and every man has a theory of his own. All business is suspended, and the soil is bereft of its tillers.

Dean's unaccountable absence caused immediate suspicion to rest upon him, and yet his friends, one and all, forced the ugly thought from their minds. Gilbert Dean a murderer, the murderer of his wife? Horrible, impossible! But the human mind easily adjusts itself to new conditions, and startling facts are readily absorbed after the first shock. "Why should Mr. Dean have mysteriously disappeared?" every one asked himself. "It looks black," was the inevitable conclusion. "But Gilbert Dean, of all men!" protested his friends. "He was the most popular man in town—rich—generous—sunny."

"There must be some explanation," reasoned the more thoughtful. "We will not damn so good a fellow as Gilbert Dean unheard."

The current of comment had turned somewhat in his favor, when it became noised about that there had been a quarrel late the previous afternoon between him and Mrs. Dean. The facts were greatly exaggerated—grotesquely distorted. In all the gossip the actress figured conspicuously. And the wrath of the town, especially the feminine portion of it, was turned towards her. Meanwhile, fortunately for Estelle, she was well away from Islington, having left on the early morning train with her company. When it became known that she had gone, gossips at once assumed that Dean had gone with her. The bitter feeling against her lessened, in a measure, the suspicion that rested on him, and many went so far as to charge her with the crime. It was established, however, at the inquest that her whereabouts could be satisfactorily accounted for during the entire time of her stay in Islington.

This bit of evidence was disappointing, and many were the narrow minds that persisted even now that she was the guilty one.

"There are witches," suggested one old woman.

"I'm sure there must be," assented her listener with a little shudder. "If there wasn't, how could there be so many mysteries?"

"And dark ones."

"Yes, and murders even."

"Oh, think of it, and this woman was an actress."

"Those actresses are just imps of the devil, that's what I think."

"Of course they are; just imps."

And thus primed, the two women separated, and each repeated the other's words to eager ears. Thus began a conception of Estelle that grew in hideousness until she was little else than a fiend incarnate in the eyes of Islington.

John Upton, the neighbor of somewhat uncertain habits, testified that he came home the night previous well on towards midnight; that just before reaching his own gate he saw Gilbert Dean on the opposite side of the street; that he was walking rapidly, and apparently had just left home.

"I called to him," said Upton, "but he didn't answer me, and he was soon beyond hearing."

There was some doubt in the minds of many about the reliability of testimony from such a source; yet, supported by that of the next witness, it made a marked impression. This witness stated that he was at the railway station at midnight; that just as the east bound train was pulling out, Gilbert Dean ran up and swung himself on the last car; that he (the witness) spoke to him as he passed, but that Dean made no response, and hurried into the car.

The witness added that he recalled now that Dean seemed a good deal agitated—a habit witnesses not infrequently have when their imagination has been quickened by the finger of suspicion.

The testimony of the last two men began to weave the noose around Dean's neck. The friends who had stood out most stoutly for him were compelled to waver. And their faith in him was still further shaken by the receipt of a telegram from the conductor of the train on which Dean left town. It stated that he had no ticket; that he paid his fare to Albany, and that he left the train at Schenectady.

There was breathless silence during the reading of this telegram, and then the people looked at one another, and pain was on their faces. "Poor Dean," they seemed to say as with one voice, and then they asked themselves what could have brought him to this—Dean, the most tender hearted man they knew.

Immediately upon receipt of the telegram from the conductor, the sheriff wired a description of Dean to Schenectady, requesting his arrest on a charge of murder.

It was three o'clock in the morning when Dean reached Schenectady. He went to a hotel near the station. He was exhausted mentally and physically alike. The strain of the last ten hours had aged him years. He walked up to his room with the step of an old man, and yet the sun had cast its cheerful glow upon the world before slumber sealed his eyes.

He slept on and on, outraged nature holding him in her recuperative grasp. At length he was awakened by a rude knocking at his door. He raised himself on his elbow and looked wildly about him. The room was strange to his eyes. Where was he, and why was he there?

Then memory served him. It all came back to him: the hideous thing he had become, the misery he had caused, the—oh, it was horrible. He covered his face with his hands as though thus he could shut out the mental vision.

There came a blow at the door that threatened to wrench it from its fastenings, and Dean answered. In another minute he was confronted by a burly officer with blue coat and brass buttons.

Dean's heart stood still. "You probably know why I am here," said the policeman gruffly.

Dean gasped. His nerves had been shaken to their very foundation.

"What—what do you want of me?" he stammered in confused reply. "What is the charge against me?"

"Murder!"

"Murder?" exclaimed Dean. "Murder?" Is she dead?" and he fell back senseless upon the bed.

XV.

IT was the day of the trial. The court room was packed to suffocation, and those who could not get inside formed groups in the halls and on the street without, all discussing the one absorbing topic.

Dean had protested his innocence from the first, but even those who had been his closest friends had their faith in him staggered, not only by the evidence brought forward at the inquest, but by his own words when apprehended in the hotel at Schenectady. What his defense would be none knew except his lawyer, Philip Wilton, a Lakefield chum of his, who had been summoned from New York to take charge of the case.

The State was represented by Amos Grymes, the district attorney, who entered upon this trial with almost savage delight. It furnished him the opportunity he had dearly craved.

He was ambitious for political advancement. What mattered it to him whether this advancement were built upon the grave of a fellow man? He had no sentiment in his cold nature. He did not know the meaning of an emotion. The conviction of Dean meant glory for him, and what was Dean to him? What was any man to him?

"Every one for himself in this world," was Grymes' creed. "The world has always been against my family—against me. I have progressed simply because I have fought the world, and now I have made a start, I'll show them that a Grymes can compel recognition."

Amos Grymes was not a comely man to look upon. He was of a stubby type, with square jaw and heavy features—almost sullen, they were. His hands were hard, with stumpy fingers. The fiber of the man was coarse. Avarice and ambition were the passions of his life. He had risen to be district attorney through the manipulation of machine politics. His strength lay with the worst element. This tragedy at the Deans' had set on fire his miserable soul. He saw at once opening before him visions of power that had hitherto seemed afar off.

A hush as of death fell upon the room when the prisoner was brought in. The most morbid of the spectators could not have imagined a change in him more awful than was the reality. There was a dullness in the eye, a languor in the carriage, a droop of the shoulders, that made him as different from the Gilbert Dean of yore as pale moonbeams differ from the radiant shafts of sunlight.

The judge entered and took his seat, a jury was sworn in, and then the clerk of the court read the indictment, charging Gilbert Dean with the murder of his wife, Louise Dartmouth Dean. Thereupon Amos Grymes stepped forth, and made a presentation of the case.

"The crime which I shall seek to bring home to its proper source," he said, among other things, "is one of peculiar atrociousness. Not the greed of gain, nor the desire of revenge, nor the stroke that seeks its victim in a moment of passion—with none of these do we have to deal. Cold, deliberate, unprovoked murder confronts us, and should the guilty one escape, through any false sympathy due to hitherto good standing in the community, it will be a blot upon the justice of the county that can never be effaced."

Grymes then proceeded to state what he proposed to prove, which was that the prisoner could not be more plainly guilty than if he had been taken red handed in the very act.

The district attorney now called the first witness, a maid in the service of Mrs. Dean. She testified that she had admitted her mistress to the house about five o'clock in the afternoon preceding the tragedy; that Mrs. Dean had seemed much disturbed in mind, and scarcely tasted of her dinner. She stated furthermore that Mr. Dean did not come home according to his custom.

"He was not in the habit, then, of staying away from this meal?" asked Grymes.

"Oh, no, sir."

"Very good," said the attorney, with such

a look of satisfaction that the poor witness came near breaking down on the stand, fearing that she had said something to convict her master.

"Will you kindly state," Grymes went on, "when was the next time you saw Mr. Dean?"

"Not till this blessed minute as I see him now afore me, God have mercy on us all."

"Never mind sentiment," snapped Grymes, adding, "But the fact that you did not see him would not prevent his having come to the house without your knowledge? He carried a latch key, did he not?"

"Yes, sir, always."

"At what time did you retire on the night of the murder?"

"About ten, sir."

"And you were roused by no noise during the night?"

"No, sir."

"Were you ever aroused by any noise in the night?"

"I can't just think now, but I suppose, sir, I have been."

"I dare say. In case a burglar had effected an entrance, you might have heard him without being sufficiently awakened to be alarmed?"

"Oh, sir, I don't know."

"Are you a light sleeper?"

"Yes, sir, I think I am."

Grymes then proceeded to another point of attack.

"When you came down stairs the next morning did you pass out by the front door for any purpose?"

"Yes, sir; to sweep off the piazza."

"Did you notice that the lock of the door had been tampered with in any way?"

"No, sir."

"And when you came to open the windows, did you find anything wrong about them?"

"No, sir."

"And was there any silver or jewelry or money missing from the house?"

"No, sir; not a thing."

This witness was then dismissed, and the cook was called, and put through an almost similar catechism. Her answers were to the same end—that no alarm was heard in the night, that nothing was missing in the morning, no locks broken, nor was there any evidence about the place to show that any stranger had been there.

A chambermaid from the Forest King House was next placed on the stand, and after testifying as to her name and occupation, had this question put to her by Grymes:

"Did you, or did you not, hear high voices coming from the ladies' parlor in the hotel on the afternoon preceding the murder?"

"I did, sir."

"Was it a man's or a woman's voice that seemed to be the most threatening?"

"A man's voice, sir."

"Could you catch what he said?"

"Yes, sir; some of it."

"Will you tell the jury what you heard?"

"Well, sir, one thing he said was, 'You shall not get away,' very savage-like."

Profound sensation in the court. Grymes' stubby mustache raised itself slightly, making about his mouth a close approach to a smile. Dean made a quick movement as if about to speak, then sank back listlessly.

"You have no means of knowing, of course," Grymes went on, "to whom this remark was addressed?"

"Yes, sir, I have," answered the witness; "because the next minute Mrs. Dean rushed out of the room like as if she had tore herself loose from somebody a holding of her."

Another sensation, and another gleam of satisfaction in the district attorney's covetous eyes.

"Did you hear anything else after Mrs. Dean had taken her departure?" he now went on.

"Yes, sir."

There was breathless silence in the court, and heads were eagerly craned not to lose a syllable of the testimony that was about to be submitted.

"Will you tell the jury what you heard? What remark did the prisoner make just after his wife had gone?"

"He said that he would find a way to silence her, that the actress woman need not be alarmed."

A low murmur of indignation swept through the court room, which was checked by the judge. Again Dean started up as if to protest, but once more sank back, with the same hopeless look in his eyes.

"What response, if any, did Miss Myrwin make to this?" proceeded Grymes.

"She spoke quite low, sir, and I could not rightly hear, but it sounded like, 'I won't be talked about in that way, Gilbert. You must defend my good name.'"

"Are you quite certain she spoke to the prisoner as 'Gilbert'?"

"Yes, sir; I heard that quite distinctly."

"What response did he make?"

"He said that it was shameful; that he didn't care whether it was his wife or not; that he was going to make her right the wrong she had done them, if it took force to do it."

"You are certain the prisoner made use of the word 'force'?"

"Yes, sir."

"What else did they say?"

"I couldn't hear all."

"Tell the jury, please, what you did hear."

"Well, there was something about her having 'made his life miserable,' that she was 'a millstone about his neck.'"

"What else did you hear?"

"Nothing else, except a noise as if he was coming out, and then we hurried to get away."

"You say 'we.' Who else was with you in the hall?"

"Johnny Crump, and Mrs. Mix, who had a room on that floor."

These two were then called to the stand in quick succession, and corroborated all that the chambermaid had said up to the point where Mrs. Dean had left the room. They had both retreated at that stage, but the boy came back in time to hear the prisoner say that somebody was a millstone about his neck.

Grymes had spent much labor upon these

witnesses. He had sought frequent interviews with them, and by patient manipulation had succeeded in molding their testimony into the shape it finally took. He next brought forward a cigar dealer who had seen Dean come out of the Forest King House at half past five.

"You are acquainted with the prisoner?" questioned Grymes.

"Yes; he has often bought cigars of me."

"Did you speak to him?"

"Yes; I said, 'Good evening, Mr. Dean.'"

"And what reply did he make?"

"None."

"Was he in the habit of ignoring you?"

"No; he was always very friendly."

"Which way did he go? Toward his home?"

"No; in the opposite direction."

"Did he appear to be walking as though he had an object in view?"

"No; sometimes he would move fast, and at others slow."

"Where did you lose sight of him?"

"At the corner of Elm and Hawk Streets,

where I turned off to go home and get my supper."

The State's next witness was a woman residing on Hawk Street, who had been standing at her gate watching for her husband to come home. She testified to seeing the prisoner pass about a quarter past six, and to thinking it strange to see him in that part of the town. Then came a farmer from Raymond Falls, who had passed Dean on the road to that village.

"Was he walking toward Raymond Falls?" asked Grymes.

"Yes."

"Was it light enough for you to be sure it was the prisoner?"

"Yes; the sun hadn't gone down yet."

"Just in what part of the road was this? Were there any houses near?"

"No; it was by that piece of woodland of Deacon Myers'."

Dr. Blauvelt was now called, and declared that he met the prisoner a few moments after the farmer had passed him.

"How do you know this?"

"Because within five minutes I overtook the farmer."

"Which way was the prisoner walking when you saw him?"

"Towards Islington."

"Then he must have turned around in the road without stopping anywhere?"

"Presumably, as there was no place for him to stop."

Another witness next testified to seeing the prisoner on Liberty Street at eight o'clock.

"In what direction was he walking?"

"Towards Raymond Falls."

"Was he walking fast or slow?"

"Slow; almost sauntering, you might say."

"Was it not dark by this time?"

"Yes."

"How then can you be certain that it was the prisoner you saw?"

"Because I met him under a street lamp."

Mrs. Hallohan, residing in a tenement opposite the Dartmouth factory, being duly sworn, stated that she had seen the prisoner enter his office in the factory, with a key, a little after eight o'clock. A constable was then called who told of meeting Dean just as he was coming down the steps from his office, somewhat after ten. Next John Upton repeated the testimony he had given at the inquest.

"Can you swear that he had just left his home?" asked Grymes.

"I am quite certain of it."

"You saw him turn out from the gate, then?"

"Yes."

"You said you spoke to him. What did you say?"

"I called out, 'Hello, you're going the wrong way!'"

"And what reply did he make?"

"None."

"Do you think he heard you?"

"He must have."

That there should be no doubt of this, Grymes now produced another witness, who had started to the station to meet a friend he expected on the midnight train.

"When did you first catch sight of the prisoner?"

"As a quick moving shadow coming down the driveway from his house."

"You say 'quick moving'; was the prisoner running?"

"I should say he was."

"But he slowed up before reaching the gate?"

"Yes."

"Do you think he saw you?"

"I don't know."

"Did you see Mr. Upton?"

"I did."

"Did you hear him call out to the prisoner as he has stated?"

"Yes."

"Where did the prisoner go then?"

"To the station, just ahead of me."

"Then what became of him?"

"He swung himself on to the last car of the Albany train, which was just moving out."

The conductor and brakeman of this train, and the night clerk from the hotel in Schenectady, were now examined, and their evidence went to show that the prisoner was in a highly nervous, almost dazed condition on the night of the murder.

But Grymes did not rest here. He fully realized the influence Dean's hitherto high standing in Islington might have upon popular opinion in the way of awakening sympathy for him. To checkmate this he had gone to Lakefield, the prisoner's native place, and by skilful maneuvering, and with untiring patience, had unearthed boyish quarrels and escapades long since forgotten by nearly all concerned in them. He brought witnesses to Islington to prove that Dean was cursed with an ungovernable temper, and that while he had always made a fair showing outwardly, his heart was black. According to these deponents, Gilbert Dean had not a spark of gratitude in his nature, lived only to gratify his senses, and had married for money.

To be sure, the men who swore to these things were rather threadbare, disreputable looking specimens of humanity themselves.

THE AFFAIR AT ISLINGTON. 177

Envy of the high estate to which their fellow townsman had attained might not have been uninfluential in inducing them to assent to Grymes' desires; but "give a dog a bad name and hang him." The astute district attorney had laboriously prepared his ground, and the seed he sowed in it instantly sprang up and bore the desired fruit.

From this phase of the accused's character Grymes passed to the affair with Marie Myrwin, the actress, with the intention of showing the actuating motive for the crime. Witnesses were brought from Albany to prove that the two were together there, and the keen scented attorney even found out about the deception Dean had practised on his wife. Eugene Illford was placed on the stand to prove it.

"You are a friend of the prisoner, I believe?" began Grymes.

"Well, a business acquaintance, say, rather."

"But you always had a high opinion of his character?"

"Yes."

"Have you any reason to suppose he deceived

his wife with regard to a visit to Albany in your company?"

"In the light of late events, I am compelled to believe that he did."

"Do you recognize this card?" went on Grymes, passing the piece of pasteboard over to him.

"Yes, it is the card I wrote at his office the day I called there and found him out."

"What did the prisoner say with regard to the card?"

"He said that he had never seen it; that it must have blown out of the window."

"Out of the office window, he meant, I presume?"

"Yes."

"And yet that card was found on Mrs. Dean's dressing table. How do you account for that?"

"I cannot account for it."

"You gathered from your call at the house, did you not, that the prisoner was not anxious to have you meet his wife?"

"Yes."

"And does this not lead you to infer that the prisoner had been leading a double life?"

" I confess I have been very much surprised in him."

While this testimony was not so directly damaging as the rest, yet, coming as it did from a friend of the accused, it had a marked effect on the jury, as tending to show the dark strain in Dean's character and his capacity for blinding the eyes of those who were about him. As the trial proceeded, and the coil of evidence circled more and more tightly about the prisoner, Grymes pursued the trail with increased ferocity. His own fame was spreading daily. His name figured prominently in all the newspapers, and " Grymes Springs a Fresh Clincher " was the heavy head line that more than once stirred his soul with a sense of triumph. He rested his side of the case with perfect confidence in the outcome.

XVI.

PHILIP WILTON, Dean's counsel, although a young man, had already established a good reputation in the metropolis. He had known Dean since they were both in knickerbockers, and had a stanch belief in his friend's innocence; but in his attempt to establish it he found himself confronted with a herculean task.

He began the defense with a well worded plea against the monstrosity of sending an innocent man to his death on circumstantial evidence, citing numerous instances where this had actually been done.

His first witnesses were some of the solid business men of Islington, who testified to Dean's integrity in every transaction they had had with him. These were followed by citizens of Lakefield, who in refutal of the stories told by the prosecution, related how Gilbert

Dean had always been, so far as they knew, an honorable, well conducted boy and man. Then came the sensational feature of the defense— Estelle's appearance on the stand.

When she entered the court room the reporters from the newspapers of three cities put fresh points to their pencils in anticipation of some particularly spicy revelations. Her face was like marble, not only in its whiteness, but in its immobility. She had known what to expect in facing such an assemblage, and had steeled herself to show no sign of the anguish that threatened to unseat her reason. Only the dire necessity of having to earn her livelihood had enabled her to play since that awful moment when she had learned of Mrs. Dean's death.

She had read the evidence brought forward at the inquest, but did not realize how black it made the case look for Gilbert till now, when she could see stony despair in the face of the man in the prisoner's dock. And yet, not one jot did her belief in his innocence abate. The Gilbert Dean she had known as boy and man simply could not commit so atrocious a crime; that was enough for her. That he could clear himself she had not an atom of doubt—till she looked upon him at this moment. There was a hopeless misery in his expression that told of ambition dead, of the extinction of all expectation of freedom.

And yet, to Estelle's eyes at least, this abandonment to despair was not the abandonment of guilt. It was simply the physical breaking down of the man beneath his terrible burden. "And it has all been through me," she told herself bitterly. "If I had not sent for him that night in Beverley, he would not have come to this!"

In spite of all her determination, her agitation when placed on the stand was pitiful. She could not but be conscious of the detestation in which she was held in Islington. Indeed, none took any pains to hide it from her.

She testified to having known the prisoner about twenty years, admitted that they had quarreled and separated, and that she had never expected to see him again until they met in the autumn.

Then, coming down to the interview with Mrs. Dean at the Forest King House, Wilton attempted to show the falseness of the testimony of the listeners in the hall.

"Just previous to Mrs. Dean's withdrawal from the room, did the prisoner say to her, 'You shall not get away'?"

"No, he did not."

"Can you recall what he did say?"

"I am not sure, but it was not that, I am certain. What he meant was, that he did not wish her to leave in that mood."

"Have you any recollection of the prisoner saying he would find a way to silence her?"

"I am sure he never said that."

"You heard the testimony of the chambermaid from the Forest King House?"

"I did."

"Now can you recall addressing the prisoner in the words of that witness: 'I won't be talked about in that way. You must defend my good name'?"

"I may have said that. I was very much agitated."

"One more question, Miss Osgood. Did the prisoner say his wife had made his life miserable, that she was a millstone about his neck?"

"No, he did not; that is wholly false."

Grymes now took up the cross examination of the actress. It was difficult for him to conceal the satisfaction he derived from this task. He knew that each question would act as a probe upon a still bleeding wound, but that inspired in him no compassion. The sentiment was foreign to his nature.

"In the direct examination," he began, "you stated your belief that the prisoner did not wish his wife to leave the room in that mood. To what mood did you refer?"

"She was very much excited."

"Can you state what had excited her?"

"The interview. She did not know that her husband and I were such old friends, and thought it strange that he should come to the hotel to see me."

"Very good. You affirmed on the direct examination that the prisoner did not say he would find a way to silence her. But two witnesses are agreed that he did say it. Now can you recollect his saying anything that was similar, some sentence with the word 'silence' in it?"

Estelle reflected an instant and then answered.

"He may have said something to the effect that the only thing we could do was to keep silent about the matter."

"That does not sound much like the words the other two witnesses testify to having heard. Do you not think that your agitation—you admitted under my opponent's examination that you were agitated—do you not think that this agitation may have weakened your memory?"

"It may have to some extent, but I am sure there was nothing threatening to Mrs. Dean said."

"But you cannot state just what was said."

"No, I cannot."

Estelle then left the stand, and a recess was

taken. Held in abhorrence as she was in the town, her testimony had added little to strengthen Dean's case. None doubted that the actress would not hesitate to perjure herself if thereby she might help the man over whom, to their eyes, she had cast her spell.

XVII.

WHEN the court reconvened, Dean himself was placed on the stand, and invited to account for his whereabouts on the night of the murder.

"At what time did you leave the Forest King House?" asked Wilton.

"About six o'clock."

"Do you recall seeing Thomas Stearns, the cigar dealer, as you came out?"

"No, I do not remember recognizing any one."

"Where did you go first?"

"Nowhere in particular. The scene with my wife had left me in a very excited frame of mind."

"But you surely have some knowledge of the direction in which you walked, have you not?"

"I only know that after I had been walking

for some time I found myself on the road to Raymond Falls."

"About what time was this?"

"Sunset; about seven o'clock."

"What did you do then? Had you any purpose in going to Raymond Falls?"

"No; I did not go there. I turned around and walked back toward town."

"Why did you take this long, purposeless walk?"

"I was trying to plan out some course of action."

"Where did you go when you reached town?"

"To my office."

"What time was this?"

"About a quarter past eight."

"Was there any one at the office besides yourself?"

"No."

"Did any one see you enter?"

"I don't know."

"What did you do after you reached your office?"

"I sat down and continued studying the problem before me."

"You had no supper, then?"

"No."

"How long did you remain in your office?"

"I do not know. I did not look at my watch."

"But you must have some idea whether it was one hour, or two, or three?"

"I should say I was there from two to three hours."

"Where did you go when you left the office?"

"Nowhere in particular. I wandered up and down the streets."

"How much time did you spend in this way?"

"Fully half an hour, I should think."

"What did you do then?"

"I went to my own home."

"Did you enter the house?"

"No."

"Why not?"

"Because I felt that I could not yet face my wife."

"How long did you remain inside the grounds?"

"I have no means of telling for certain."

"Were there any lights in the house?"

"Yes, there was a light in the dining room."

"What did you do next?"

"I heard the whistle of the midnight train, and I suddenly determined to go to the station and board it."

"Had you any object in mind in thus leaving town?"

"None in particular. I was still dazed by the affair at the hotel. I was restless and excited, scarcely accountable for what I did."

"Did you run from the house to the gate?"

"I started to, as I feared I might miss the train. Then I remembered that it did not matter so very much if I did miss it."

"Did you see any one as you passed out at the gate?"

"Yes; I saw a man across the street."

"Did you recognize him?"

"Not until he spoke. Then I knew it was John Upton."

"Why did you not reply?"

"Because I was not in a mood for conversation."

"Had you any idea where you would go when you boarded the train?"

"No; I simply wanted to get away from the place where I had been through so much misery."

"You did not stop to purchase a ticket, then?"

"No."

"What did you say to the conductor when he came through?"

"I told him I wanted to pay my way to Albany, as I had had no time to buy a ticket."

"You then left the train at Schenectady. Why did you do this?"

"For no special reason. A man is liable to do unaccountable things after he has been told by his wife that she does not wish to have anything more to do with him."

There was a rustling all over the court room at this point in the proceedings.

"When the officers entered your room at

the hotel the next morning," Wilton went on, "and announced that you were wanted on a charge of murder, why did you exclaim, 'Is she dead?'"

"When I heard the word 'murder' from the officer's lips, the horrible thought flashed over me that an awful evil had befallen my wife."

Grymes now took up the cross examination of the prisoner.

"When you left the Forest King House," he asked, "did you not at first walk at a rather fast gait?"

"I may have done so. I do not fully recall the speed at which I moved."

"And the direction in which you at first turned would have taken you to your own home, would it not?"

"Yes."

"Can you give the jury any reason why you walked toward Raymond Falls?"

"No reason except that I was very much disturbed in mind, and did not care where I went."

"You were thinking of your wife, I presume?"

"Yes."

"And it occurred to you, doubtless, that things might have been much more harmonious had she not called on Miss Osgood that afternoon?"

"Yes."

"This, then," Grymes went on, "accounted for your perturbed feelings?"

"Yes."

"You say you cannot account for your walking toward Raymond Falls; can you give any explanation of your suddenly ceasing to go in that direction, and turning back toward Islington?"

"No, I cannot, beyond what I have already said about my state of mind."

"You were still thinking about your wife, I presume?"

"Yes."

"Do you recall coming to some sudden decision in regard to your course of action at the moment when you turned in your tracks?"

Grymes looked very intently at the prisoner as he put this question.

Dean reflected an instant before replying, and then answered, "No."

"But there must have been some cause to induce you to turn about at that particular point?" persisted Grymes.

"There may have been, but my brain was in such a distracted condition at the time that I have lost all memory of it," replied Dean wearily.

"When you went to your office," the district attorney proceeded, "did you have a light there?"

"No."

"Were you in the habit of going to your office in the evening and sitting in the dark to meditate?"

"No."

"If you heard of another man doing it, would you not think it strange, not to say ridiculous?"

"I suppose I should."

"You have said that your occupation at the

office was to continue the study of the problem before you. Will you state to the court the nature of this problem?"

There was an instant's silence during which the traditional pin might have been heard had it fallen to the floor. Then Dean replied:

"My wife had misunderstood my motives, and I was endeavoring to reason out the proper course to take in order to justify myself in her eyes."

Profound sensation in the court room.

"When you waited till about eleven o'clock to return to your own home," resumed Grymes, "did you have any special object in this delay?"

"No; I had not thought till then about going back at all."

"At what time were your servants in the habit of shutting up the house and going to bed?"

"At ten o'clock."

"You have stated that you saw a light in your dining room. Did it not occur to you as strange at that hour?"

"No; I merely supposed that my wife was still sitting up."

"Were you in the habit of occupying the dining room as a sitting room?"

"We sometimes remained there in the evening."

"Would you not consider it strange in a husband to come to his house after eleven at night and approach to within a few feet of the room where he knew his wife was awaiting him, then turn about suddenly and hurry away?"

"I might as a general thing, but in my own case I had no reason for supposing that my wife was awaiting me."

"You admit, then, that you had parted in anger?"

"No; there was only a misunderstanding between us."

"A misunderstanding that you believed you could not explain away, otherwise you would not have turned about and rushed off to catch that train. Is this what the court is to conclude?"

"No; I could explain it away. My wife was wrong."

"Why, then, did you not go in and convince her of the fact?"

"Because I had already endeavored to do so, and failed."

"Yet you knew this when you came back to your house. You must have changed your mind suddenly!"

"I did."

"Without any special reason for it?"

"None except that the hopelessness of the task just at that time came over me with convincing power."

"Then you are inclined to believe that had you entered the dining room, and proceeded to argue the matter with her, she would not have taken it kindly?"

"I have no belief in the matter."

"Then perhaps you have some knowledge?"

"No; I cannot make any statement as to what would have been the outcome of an interview that did not take place."

"And yet you have said that the hopelessness of trying to convince your wife that she had wronged you, was what caused you to leave the grounds. Is not this equivalent to admitting that an interview at the time would have been of a somewhat distressing nature?"

"I suppose it is, but as there was no interview, I do not see of what importance any guesswork on my part as to its nature can be."

But Grymes did. He asked no more questions. He seemed perfectly content with what he had already learned. The case was then adjourned to permit of a summing up of the evidence.

The affair aroused widespread comment. Dailies in the big cities devoted columns to an account of the trial as it progressed from day to day, and in Islington itself it formed the chief topic of discussion, although this is scarcely the word where all were agreed in one opinion. In fact, it had been a matter of extreme difficulty to make up the jury, so outspoken were the townspeople in their views of Dean's conduct.

Some freely expressed themselves to the effect that it was a waste of the county's money to go through the form of a trial. "In some towns of the Southwest," they added suggestively, " short work would be made with such as he."

Sometimes Wilton wondered whether his client would be safe even should the law pronounce him guiltless.

XVIII.

DEAN'S lawyer made an earnest effort to save him. He summed up all the testimony that had been brought against his client, and then proceeded to show that it was coincidental, not incriminating, facts that were seeking to hurry the prisoner to the death chair.

"In the fascination of adjusting about its victim the coil of circumstantial evidence," he proceeded, " the prosecution has become blind to the light of reason. It has contradicted itself. After carefully collecting witnesses to prove the prisoner to be possessed of ungovernable temper, in the heat of which any crime may have been committed, it then as carefully seeks to show that the deed with which my client was charged, was committed with the most fiendish deliberation. According to the character the distinguished attorney for the prosecution has given to the prisoner, the time for him to have perpetrated the murder was at the Forest King House, when, according to the evidence supplied by the same source, the most direful threats were uttered against the deceased. I need not remind you that this evidence was shown to be misleading, proving that no threats of this description were made.

"What, then, are you asked to do, gentlemen of the jury? To send a man to the electric chair because his wife died a violent death some eight hours after she had quarreled with him. Not the faintest trace of direct proof is brought against him, not even the fact that he was in the same house when she died. No doubt my opponent will endeavor to convince you that the prisoner must have committed the deed because there was nothing to show that anybody else had done it. But is this the sort of reasoning on which to take from a man his life?

"Granting for one instant that the prisoner, after the calm deliberation which the opposition has shown he exercised, did take the life of the deceased, what would he gain thereby? Doubtless the prosecution will tell you that it was to remove the obstacle to his union with some one else. But is not such a supposition illogical on the face of it? A man who would risk putting his life in jeopardy to remove an obstacle to a new marriage would not hesitate to gain his end by a less hazardous course. Now, gentlemen of the jury, disabuse your minds of a crime that everything seems to point to; think only of the facts which exist, as they have been presented to you, and see if in them you can find one single circumstance that will convince you that my client has been guilty of the most atrocious of crimes."

A deep hush succeeded Wilton's plea. Every one present felt the solemnity of the moment. Then Grymes rose, slowly, with the air of a man fully convinced of his position in the estimation of his fellow men, and who was therefore in no hurry to reassert it.

"Your honor and gentlemen of the jury,"

he began, with the same deliberation in his speech, "we are here on serious business. I feel called upon to remind you of this fact because I have feared that the words of my predecessor may have misled you. Arguments that partake of so childish a tinge are apt to throw one's mind off the true purport of the affair upon which we are now engaged. This is seeing to it that justice be done, without fear or favor. Sentimentality has no place in the problem; to judge from the words of my predecessor, one might think that you, gentlemen of the jury, had each a personal spite against the prisoner, which you were determined to gratify by bringing him in guilty. For my part, I ask you to look at nothing, to consider nothing, but the evidence which has been brought before you. Here is a man who has been leading a double life for months previous to the commission of the crime with which he is now charged. He has not disputed that fact. On the very afternoon of the murder he quarrels with the deceased; this fact is not denied by the defense.

My colleague tells you that the line of argument of the prosecution is contradictory because it seeks to prove, in one instance, that the prisoner is of quick temper, and in another shows that the awful deed was committed after calm deliberation. But have you never heard of nursing wrath? The fire to the train of powder was set during that interview in the hotel. It crept slowly, slowly along the line toward culmination during those walks in and about the town whose apparent aimlessness the prisoner himself confesses he cannot explain.

"My learned brother mentions the fact that it has not been proven that the prisoner was in the house at the time the murder was committed. The puerility of this subterfuge only shows the weakness of his case. The accused has admitted being within the grounds; we scarcely expect him, inasmuch as he has pleaded 'Not guilty,' to stand forth and acknowledge that he really strangled the deceased. But he had said in your hearing that an interview with his wife at that hour would have been a stormy one. The spark, lighted at the Forest King House, had been finding its way along the devious turnings of the powder train till all it needed was the touch of the powder itself to burst forth into a mighty explosion.

"Then mark the actions of the accused after leaving his home. He started to run at first; then, seeing passersby, slowed down, with that fear of awakening suspicion which is the surest indication of guilt. He avoids answering the salutations of friends, boards a midnight train just as it is moving out of the station, pays his fare to one place and gets off at another, and when finally he is charged with murder, his accusing conscience leaps impulsively from his lips in the query, 'Is she dead?'

"This may be circumstantial evidence, but if we had more, what need would there be of a trial?

"One point more; my learned brother of the opposition has declared that not sufficient motive has existed for the crime; he has intimated that a man would prefer to commit bigamy to murder. Perhaps a person of another disposition might have done this; but as the prisoner has himself stated, he is a man of impulse. To such a one, murder—a deed that may be committed in an instant—comes more natural than the deliberately planned abandonment of one woman and the fleeing with another. Of what was he thinking during those long and aimless walks? He did not tell us, but it was evidently not of seeking consolation with her who was the cause of the estrangement between himself and his wife, else he would have gone to her.

"Let us sum up the whole case in a nutshell. Our town is shocked with a murder whose hideousness calls loudly for vengeance on the perpetrator. There is not the faintest indication that it was committed by housebreakers; there is every indication that it was done by the husband whose evil deeds the wife had just brought home to him. Had the affair occurred in Angel Alley or Paradise Court, I wager that there would have been scant hesitation in bringing the guilty one to book. But because the prisoner resides on Berkeley Hill, because he has wealth and position, and has hitherto shown only his smooth side to the community, heaven and earth are moved to set him free. It will be a lasting blot upon the county, I contend, if this be done. What, shall wealth get exemption where poverty receives only its just due? The eyes of half the country are on this town today; countless telegraph instruments stand ready to click out the news of your decision. Those who contemplate dark crimes, it may be, hinge their final determination on what shall be the verdict here. Remember these facts, and render your report in accordance with them."

Grymes sat down amid a buzz of excited comment, which ceased quickly as order was demanded, and the judge began to speak. But it was not to give his charge to the jury; he announced instead that he would reserve this for the next morning, till which time the case would stand adjourned.

XIX.

"IT is going to be against us, Phil; I feel sure of that."

Dean's voice was calm, but his handclasp was not so steady as it usually was when he welcomed his old time chum to his quarters in the jail.

"If it does, I'll appeal for a new trial. I feel certain I can get it. Why, a friend of yours is waiting outside now to see you. He says he has not communicated with you before; but he has been working for you all the time."

"Who is it?"

"Ford; Thomas T. Ford," replied Wilton. "He has come all the way from Kansas City expressly to render you all the aid he can."

Dean's face went white. He had not thought to hear from the Fords now. Jessie was a cousin of Louise. What did Tom mean by coming to see him? Dean had heard nothing from him since that memorable visit to his Western home. It seemed like a Nemesis that he should turn up at this crisis.

"Bring him here, and then leave us alone for a little while, will you, Phil?" and when the other had gone, Dean steeled himself for an ordeal he dreaded more than he did the scene in court on the morrow.

But Ford's greeting was altogether different from what he had expected. "Gilbert, old man!" he exclaimed, with a pressure of the hand that meant so much of friendship where only contempt had been awaited, that Dean was closer to being unnerved than during his whole awful experience.

"Then you do not believe, Tom——" he began, when Ford interrupted him with—"I believe only this, my dear fellow: that you have been out of your mind for more than a year past, and that you are no more responsible for what you may have done within that period than a marble statue would be."

"What do you mean?" gasped Dean, looking at him with new horror in his eyes.

"Listen: you remember your last visit to our home?"

"Only too distinctly," said Dean in a tone scarcely audible.

"Well, you certainly did not deport yourself on that occasion like a sane being."

"Then you did see me with—*her?*"

"To be sure I did, and thought the worse of you till your inexplicable conduct afterwards convinced me that you were not to be held accountable for your acts. I am surprised that your lawyer has not seen matters in this light before."

Dean went up to his friend, put an arm on either shoulder, and looked straight into his eyes.

"Tom," he said, "what is the undercurrent to all this? You must know perfectly well that I deliberately tried to deceive you that night. I was a bungler, I admit, but my attempt was made in the full light of reason. God knows I have freely admitted the folly of my course up to a certain point——"

"Ah, that is just it!" broke in Ford. "You

have been such a half way offender throughout this whole miserable business that there is but one conclusion to arrive at, and that one is the only thing that will save you from a shameful death. With infinite pains I have tracked your every movement that night in our city, and——"

"Then you discovered nothing that was really criminal in any one of them, for there was nothing."

"The very point I wish to make. Don't you catch my meaning, man? You had labored as though to produce a mountain, and brought forth a mouse. It was the same in Albany—for I have taken pains to push investigation there, too—and——"

"Stop!" cried Dean hoarsely. "I see what you mean now, and were it to save me from ten thousand executions, I would not permit such a defense. Drag *her* name into this wretched affair again, and in such a light! I would first——"

"But you are clearing her name completely, man," the other broke in.

"Only so far as I myself am concerned; it leaves it smirched by inference to the end of time. Would you have me crown my folly by an act of cowardice so base that there would be no hole on earth deep enough to hide me?"

"Then you will go to the death chair, Gilbert Dean, as surely as the sun will rise tomorrow. No jury on earth will acquit you in the face of the evidence submitted."

"If I die because I refuse to live on such terms, I die more nobly than I have lived. Ah, Tom, through deception I have already seared my soul as with a red hot iron. The wounds still bleed. I have done more evil in the world than there is time in eternity to atone for. I will not say, do not tempt me, for it is no temptation."

"But if you will not think of yourself, bestow some thought on your friends, on your family, on the family of poor Louise. If they prove you *non compos mentis*, not only are you absolved from paying the penalty for her death, but all your demeanor toward her will appear in a different light. Surely this view of the case demands some consideration from you."

"Nothing you can say will change me, Tom. I know you mean it all in friendship, and don't think I do not appreciate your coming here now and taking my hand as you have done. I can't think you would do this if you really believed that I deserved the verdict which you tell me the jury will bring in tomorrow."

It was now Ford's turn to look Dean straight in the eyes—eyes which did not flinch beneath the penetrating gaze.

"Hang it, man, you wouldn't harm a fly! I *know* that, and yet——"

"And yet what?"

"Why must you meet this awful death when you don't deserve it?"

"Perhaps it is best, Tom. What would life be worth to me now? But your time is up. Good by and promise me that you will make no attempt on the line you have suggested."

"I promise, Gilbert." They shook hands and Ford went off with the warden.

Dean sat there stolidly for a few moments, thinking over the interview.

"He believes that I am guilty," he finally ejaculated. "And God help me, so do they all!"

XX.

DEAN'S doom was sealed. He had been convicted of murder in the first degree. The jury were out but a few moments. In their eyes, as well as in the eyes of the people, it was clear that Dean had murdered his wife. His counsel's efforts to obtain a new trial were unavailing. The day was set for his removal to Auburn, and the week in which he was to die had already been named.

Estelle had come to Islington that she might be near him and with him to the last. She saw him but once. She found him broken down. He was an old man now. The steel of self accusation entered her soul when he came up to those cruel dividing bars and put his fingers through for her to touch.

"Can you forgive me, Gilbert?" she whispered, her eyes streaming.

"Forgive you, Estelle?" he repeated.

"There is nothing to forgive. You are stainless, as I am stainless of that awful crime with which I am charged. If I had heeded you, I should not have laid myself open to the suspicion."

"But if I had not come into your life again, you would never have been brought to this."

"I am not so sure of that. My marriage with Louise was an unhallowed one. I did not love her as I should have done, as she was deserving of being loved. These matters always adjust themselves. In our case fate used you as the means. You are not to blame. God knows you warned me often enough of the folly of my course."

"But I ought to have gone away, Gilbert; gone somewhere out of the country, where you would never have found me."

"No, Estelle, your going away could not have altered my feelings for you. If there were sin in loving you, that sin was mine, not yours. For that I am willing to answer. We know, both of us, that it was a pure love, not the sinful one poor Louise believed it.

That is where I have wronged *you*, Estelle. I have made it possible for the world to say that of you which is false, but which you are powerless to disprove. Can you forgive me for that?"

"A thousand times, dear. But let us not speak of that. I have come to cheer you as to the future, not to lament the past. I am working to save you, others are working. There is yet time. You will be set free. Only keep up heart."

"That is like you, Estelle, to be a comforter. But the hope is vain. Only tell me one thing, that in your inmost heart you do not believe me——"

"Hush, hush! How can you suggest such a thing? You know I believe in you as I believe in my own life."

"Then God is good to me, very good, after all."

The keeper now touched Estelle on the arm to remind her that her time was up. She had not strength to say good by, could only murmur, "I will come again," as she pressed her lips to his finger tips. Then the jailer helped her from the corridor, only to see her faint in Wilton's arms.

That same night a letter was brought to her at her hotel. It was addressed in a strange hand. When she opened it, a stony look of horror came into her eyes.

A WARNING.

Unless you leave Islington within twenty four hours from this date you will be dealt with summarily. There will be no favors shown you because you are not a man. Islington shall not harbor the mistress of a murderer.

(Signed) WHITE CAPS.

Estelle sat mute for an instant, the sheet shaking in her hand. Its every word stung her to the quick. To be sure, it was an anonymous communication, and as such deserved to be treated with contempt; but that it should have entered the mind of any one to write it was where the anguish lay.

Once more she read the cruel words. They seemed to fascinate her as the glance of the serpent lures the helpless bird. "Heaven is merciful in one thing," she murmured; "that it keeps from us the knowledge of what the future holds. How could I have lived my life knowing this was to be part of it?"

But presently a new mood seized her. Her eyes flashed, and she sprang from her seat, crumpling the letter in her hand.

"They shall not send me from him," she cried. "I will stay. They dare not touch me!"

She sent for Wilton.

"Read that," she said, handing him the note. "Cannot the writers be found and made answerable for their audacity?"

The lawyer's face paled as he took in the full purport of the communication. He had heard ugly rumors about the town. He knew that the affair was no trifling one.

"You must leave Islington at once," he said.

"What!" exclaimed Estelle. "Go away without seeing Gilbert again? It would seem cowardly. I am not afraid."

"Your staying can do no good. Indeed, it will rather weaken whatever faint chances Gilbert might have. Besides, if he hears of this, his anxiety for your safety will only torment him. These fiends are capable of anything."

"But I cannot go without bidding Gilbert good by. Surely the enmity of one or two people in the town will not harm me."

"It is not one or two, Estelle."

"But even were it a hundred, I will not let them see that they can frighten me. I came here to be with Gilbert. If the prison authorities allow me to see him, I see no reason why I should stay away."

Wilton protested, and then said that he would go out to learn the temper of the people.

Estelle had arranged to visit the jail again at ten o'clock the next morning, but before she had finished her breakfast Wilton appeared.

"You must go away on the 9:40," he said. "The sentiment in the town is very pronounced, and is growing more threatening every hour, as the fact of your being here spreads. Remember, it is for Gilbert's sake as well as your own."

"But I must see him again," Estelle pleaded.

"It would be suicidal," the lawyer interposed. " Besides, you have not time."

Much against her will, Estelle was finally persuaded to act on this suggestion. Leaving without seeing Gilbert, and with the knowledge that she would never see him again, was agonizing. But that her going away was wise, she was herself convinced after she was on the train. Dark looks were cast at her as she went with Wilton to the station, and now and then a jeering remark reached her ears. It was all like some awful nightmare. Had it not been for the lawyer's presence, she knew not what insult might have been offered her. As it was, after her departure, Wilton himself barely escaped rough handling because of his championship of her cause.

Meantime Dean was removed to Auburn. He was perfectly passive. Some of those with whom he came in contact declared that he did not yet fully realize the horror of his position; others, among them Wilton, affirmed that he exhibited no sign of dread or despair simply because he had suffered all that he could suffer when the murder of his wife was first laid at his door.

One by one his last days on earth were notched off; but the chaplain of the prison, who had more frequent intercourse with him than any one else, could note no increase of nervousness as the fatal date drew near. Dean was friendly with him at all times, except when urged to free his soul by confession.

"Why should I confess to a lie?" he asked. "Sins I have committed—many of them. For these I most humbly do crave pardon, but of that great sin for which I am to die, I am innocent."

Earnestly the chaplain pleaded with him to recede from a position which could avail him nothing in this world, and only jeopardized his chances of happiness in the next. "I am innocent," Dean would repeat, not violently, but with a calmness that almost convinced the priest in face of the glaring evidence piled up against him.

At last the chaplain ceased to speak of the matter, and then Dean opened his heart more fully to him. He was a young man, and this fact gave the condemned one a feeling that his own weaknesses could find more ready palliation than with one whose own youth, with its follies, was far back in the past.

"It is not so hard for me to die," Dean said to him, shortly before the end. "If it were not that my death would seem to justify so many in the belief that I am what the court has decreed me to be, I would go gladly. Life was never really a boon to me after I found out that I loved some one else better than my wife. My nature is too finely organized to live recklessly. I could never abandon myself to evil courses as most men can. It was impossible for me to forget that I was transgressing. Others remember only afterwards in the form of remorse. With me the pain was mingled with the pleasure. I felt myself to be a brute even while I was planning to be still more brutish. Punishment for that I deserve. If my condemnation only read, 'You are to die, for deceiving your wife,' I should not murmur, because it would be just."

The last day came. In some way the reporters had ascertained the date of the execution, and an elaborate arrangement of signals was in readiness to convey to the ends of the country the intelligence that Islington's wife murderer had met with his deserts.

It was on this final morning that the chaplain made his last attempt to extract a confession from Dean.

"No," was the firm reply; "I will not die with a lie upon my lips. But I blame no one; it is my own folly that has brought me where I am. 'As ye sow, so must ye reap,' and if I have sowed only foolish weakness and reap the penalty for the most awful of crimes, it is a pity, but I must submit to the rulings of a higher will than mine. Men may never find out their mistake; but God knows. Aye, and there is one on earth who believes in me, too."

"Not her name," implored the chaplain. "Do not let her name be the last thing on your lips."

"And why should it not be? She is as

pure as an angel in heaven. I have ruined her life. It is as little as I can do to give her the poor comfort of knowing that I went to my death with the thought of her to make me brave. Come, are they not ready for me now?"

With steady step he walked into the chamber from which a few minutes later was borne forth the rigid body of one who met nobly an ignoble death.

XXI.

WHEN Estelle left Islington under such fearful circumstances, it seemed as if she must give way to utter despair. If she had only been permitted to see Gilbert once again, she felt that she could better endure her lot. But to realize that she had been deliberately driven from his side, was execrated by an entire community, among whom she would never dare venture again—the recollections of all this oppressed her with a sense of horror from which she could not escape.

The words of that "warning" were burned indelibly into her brain. Waking, she thought of them always; sleeping, they took living shape and tormented her in the form of demons who had vowed never to let her rest. The fictitious strength that had carried her through so much, gave way at last. One morning she found she could not leave her bed. She had scarcely power to speak or to raise her hand. And yet her mind seemed tirelessly active—going over and over again the scenes of that last day in Islington, repeating endlessly the contents of that letter.

Her tortured fancy pictured her as being compelled to return to the town, as walking through its streets—the butt of ridicule, the target for jeers, the object at which the universal finger of scorn was pointed. All unbidden, there came visions of little children being taught to shield their eyes from the sight of her; of women holding aside their skirts as she passed; of men nudging one another and saying, "There she goes," in the familiar tone that embodies the utmost limits of contempt.

She could think of nothing else. Full of Gilbert as her heart was, each thought of him only reminded her afresh of her humiliation. But one hope sustained her. She knew that Wilton was still working faithfully for him; if only he could be saved, she cared not what fate overtook herself.

And so the days passed by. Each morning and evening she had the paper brought to her, and turned with feverish eagerness to see whether a reprieve had been granted. But there was nothing to reward her, only now and then an item stating that wife murderer Dean still stoutly maintained his innocence. And then one morning she read the lines, "Gilbert Dean Pays the Full Penalty for His Crime."

He was dead; murdered, as truly as was poor Louise. Nothing that she might ever do could bring him back to her. His innocence might be established fifty times over, but it would be all one to him now. He had gone out from her life forever, and she was left alone, alone to fight those horrible shapes, that now, waking as well as sleeping, were always pursuing her.

"Gilbert," she cried, "why do you not come to me? There are men with white masks over their faces. They are driving me before them. I have no rest. Save me, save me!"

Her voice rose shrill. Some of the servants in the house where she was staying heard her and hastened to the room. She gazed at them as though she had never seen them before. There was a wildness in her eyes that terrified them. A doctor was hastily summoned.

"It is here," he said gravely, touching his forehead.

After a week or two, as there was no change, a commission was appointed. She was examined and adjudged insane. But she was quite passive, and allowed them to do with her what they would.

One day Wilton read in the papers that Marie Myrwin, the actress so unpleasantly associated with the Dean murder, had gone out of her mind, and had been placed in confinement.

"Poor Estelle," he murmured. "God forgive me for wishing that it had been death instead."

He lost no time in going to see her, and arranging that she should be made as comfortable as possible. She knew him, but only as she had known him when he and Gilbert and herself had been young people together in Lakefield.

"Gilbert has not been to see me in a long while, Phil," she said. "Why doesn't he come? Perhaps, though, he doesn't know how much I love him."

"Is there no hope?" Wilton asked the doctor.

"None," was the reply.

He saw her again before he went away. This time she seemed to have more comprehension of the real nature of the things that had befallen.

"You shall not kill him," she moaned. "He never murdered her! But she was cruel to me. He would not harm her for it. Gilbert, Gilbert, why do you sit there, helpless, looking at them? They will kill you. I see it in their eyes."

"God help her," Wilton murmured, as he went his way; "she is beyond the help of man."

XXII.

FOR many months the Dartmouth property in Islington, where the Deans had lived, stood idle. It had fallen to the heritage of some relations of Mrs. Dean who resided in a distant State. They had no idea of coming to live there themselves, and while the awful associations that clung about the house were still so fresh in all minds, it was a difficult matter to find a purchaser. But as time passed by, and after some mineral springs were discovered in the neighborhood, a syndicate was formed which bought in the property, and set about putting up a big summer hotel on the site. Spring was just opening again when the house was unlocked to admit of the furniture being removed.

The Islington *Journal* not long afterwards, under startling headlines, contained the following:

A most shocking miscarriage of justice has been brought to light. It seems that Gibert Dean, who was electrocuted last fall for the murder of his wife, was innocent of the crime. Mrs. Dean committed suicide by taking poison. After a thorough investigation this paper is enabled to give the facts in a case which only proves anew the fatal weakness of circumstantial evidence in criminal trials.

Among the articles of furniture in the Dean dining room was a sideboard of rather peculiar construction. Built of oak and exceedingly heavy, it did not sit flush with the carpet, but rested about an inch above it on four claw feet. When this sideboard was moved out from its place against the wall during the recent sale of effects, a litter of rubbish was discovered to be beneath it, as its nearness to the floor prevented the introduction of broom or brush. There was a silver knife, a penholder, a nickel match safe, and a bit of crumpled writing paper.

On picking up the latter and smoothing it out, a workman discovered writing on it, in pencil. In brief, it was a note in Mrs. Dean's hand, as has been proven beyond all doubt. We give herewith the contents:

I can endure this agony no longer. In spite of all that I have seen with my own eyes, I love my husband still. But to love him and know him to be false to me is anguish too keen for mortal to bear. I have taken poison. Soon all will be over. I want Gilbert to know that I forgive him for all that he has made me suffer. If my death will make him happy, he shall have the opportunity to taste of the joy it seems I could not give him. Perhaps I have sinned in what I have done. If I have, there is no remorse in my heart. There is room there only for love—love and sorrow. Dying I injure no one, myself least of all, for to live after what has happened would be daily torture. I write this that the world may know I alone——

Here the note broke off abruptly. The writing, steady at first, shows traces, as it proceeds, of a shaking hand, until at the last it is scarcely legible. Undoubtedly this was caused by the working of the poison, which had taken effect sooner than the writer had imagined it would. As the final seizure overcame her, it is probable that Mrs. Dean crumpled the note tightly in her hand, before clutching at her throat in the death agony; then, as she fell, the paper dropped from her nerveless fingers close to the sideboard, underneath which it might have slid at once, or been kicked there unknowingly by some of the servants in the next morning's excitement.

Could there be a more shocking arraignment of the injustice of securing so called justice by means of circumstantial evidence?

As soon as the facts above set forth were established even to Amos Grymes' grudging satisfaction, Wilton hastened to Estelle in the hope that she might be made to comprehend the happy, if tardy truth. But he saw at once that hope was vain. Her mind was as full of shadows as on his previous visit, and he came away with her last words echoing again hauntingly in his ears: "Gilbert, Gilbert, why do you sit there, helpless, looking at them? They will kill you. I see it in their eyes."

THE END.

www.ingramcontent.com/pod-product-compliance
Lightning Source LLC
Chambersburg PA
CBHW021809230426
43669CB00008B/680